# BECOME A SUCCESSFUL RESIDENTIAL SUBDIVISION DEVELOPER

## The Expert Advice You Must Have

KEVIN J. KENNY

LAND DEVELOPMENT ADVISORS USA PRESS

**ISBN: 978-0-578-27418-8**

I dedicate this book to my three daughters, Keisha Marie, Brianna Cathleen, and Caitlin Peggy-Eileen, each is always in my thoughts though separated by distance. May the distance disappear.

# ABOUT THE AUTHOR

Kevin J. Kenny is a retired Connecticut professional land surveyor and residential subdivision developer. He had a consultant practice for 31 years primarily designing residential subdivisions for developers in south central Connecticut, and individually or in partnership developed residential subdivisions in the same area for 37 years. He is an expert in land development and was so respected that the Town of Guilford where he resided, twice called upon him to become involved in municipal land use regulations.

He was invited to join as the only individual not a member of the municipal land use staff the ad hoc committee charged with writing the initial proposed subdivision regulation for the Planning and Zoning Commission for Open Space Subdivision Development. It was his professional advice in land use and its development that resulted in a quick adoption of the regulation by the Planning and Zoning Commission. Since its adoption it has demonstrated its success in maximizing the dedicated open space area of all subsequent subdivisions, with the bonus of maintaining the property owners and developers' goal of the same lot yield as a standard subdivision. It has continuously proved to create very substantial open space areas in subdivisions, with many such areas adjoining similar created open space in adjoining subdivisions besides reducing infrastructure, a benefit for both the developer and the town.

Subsequently, to the regulation adoption he created a personal open space development subdivision, the first for Guilford, its success was quickly followed by similar subdivisions by many other developers.

Also, as the vice chairperson of the Guilford Zoning Board of Appeals he wrote the first comprehensive regulation and standards for applicants requesting a variance of a zoning regulation, ending the "hodge-podge" of poorly documented applications generally prepared by the layperson applicant. Simpler variance requests could often now be prepared by a diligent layperson following the new regulations and standards, with professional consultants and attorneys focusing on complex variance applications.

He was a participant and eventually a co-author in a working seminar researching Connecticut boundary law held at the Yale University Law School, resulting in the publication of, "Madson, On Connecticut Real Property Boundary Law, by T.S. Madson II, 1989, LSS Publishing Company".

Finally, he created and owns Land Development Advisors USA, a website advisory resource for homebuilders, experienced subdivision developers and investors, advising them in how to have success in developing residential subdivisions.

# TABLE OF CONTENTS

# INTRODUCTION

Mu book focuses on the first-time developer although established developers will also find it beneficial. By presenting information concisely, one can quickly understand every topic of my book. For the initial developer, the skills obtained will allow you to move onto your first subdivision project in the minimal amount of time.

The purpose of this book now that I am retired, is to provide others with the expertise I gained from both my consultant practice and businesses developing subdivisions in Connecticut. As a consultant I designed subdivisions for numerous developers for over three decades while also developing my own subdivisions for nearly four decades.

I have found that most people mistakenly believe that only monied people or home-builders have the capability to become subdivision developers, that perception is untrue, I know that as a fact, just read Chapter Zero which follows to be convinced.

This book is the A-to-Z information source for residential subdivision development. It is concise, providing the most valuable information for you doing a first project and subsequent ones.

If this is your first subdivision, my recommendation is that you especially focus your attention on, **Chapter Zero through Chapter Six – Part One, and Chapters Ten, Twelve and Thirteen**, the key chapters for a first-time developer.

When you eventually move onto larger subdivision projects with road and other infrastructure construction, it is time to read the other chapters if you haven't already done so, they focus on those development elements, plus other less frequent development matters that may occasionally arise.

I strongly recommend that your initial subdivision project be of small size with no public services, without the need for building a road, as this will reduce the time required for site investigations, design of the subdivision, and minimize the expenses necessary to get your subdivision approved

The Appendix contains twelve typical municipal forms and reference maps associated with developing subdivisions, familiarize yourself with them as they and possibly other such forms and mapping will be part of your career as a subdivision developer.

So, get going to financial success.

# CHAPTER ZERO (P.O.B.)

## HOW THE AUTHOR BECAME A SUBDIVISION DEVELOPER AND MORE IMPORTANTLY HOW YOU CAN ALSO DO IT

### P.O.B. – POINT OF BEGINNING

The title of the first topic, P.O.B. is a land surveyor's designation of the starting point when evaluating a survey map, as to the accuracy of its geometry describing the boundary lines of the property.

Chapter Zero was created specifically to be your P.O.B. before commencing your reading of the topics on subdivision development contained in the 17 chapters of this book

My hope is that by reading about how I became a developer of subdivisions that it will ease any concerns you may have as to whether your becoming a developer is pie-in-the-sky dreaming or potentially real. Let me assure you that it is real. The basic key to success in becoming a subdivision developer revolves around two things, reading this book to obtain the needed knowledge, and then moving forward with an action plan to obtain the goal of creating your first subdivision.

So let us begin your journey.

### WHY I BEGAN AS A SUBDIVISION DEVELOPER

As a young married couple in the mid 1970's expecting our first child, we were living in a rented apartment in New Haven, Connecticut. I was a survey technician with one of the largest engineering and surveying firms in southern Connecticut, my wife was a registered nurse at a local hospital. We had saved a modest amount of money for a down payment towards a single-family house, and were looking in the suburbs, specifically in the area referred to as the East Shore towns, the several towns east of New Haven fronting on Long Island Sound, one of which was the Town of Guilford, our favorite.

We eventually chose Guilford, a town settled in 1639 with the third highest number of surviving colonial homes in the U.S. It has a large geographic area and in the 1970's had a modest though growing population due to the opening of the Connecticut Turnpike

(I-95) in 1958. That opening resulted in continuous construction of residential subdivisions up to when we began looking in 1974.

Most homes being built were large 8 and 9 room colonial style homes, our style of home, but as it turned out, requiring a higher down payment than our savings permitted, and an uncomfortable monthly mortgage payment. So, we decided it was prudent to look for a smaller less expensive home as a starter, but we were soon disappointed by what was available, so we decided not to buy, instead to continue saving for that colonial home for a couple of years.

A few months later I discussed with my wife an alternative, instead of waiting two years while continuing to save, begin looking for a small tract of land to subdivide, sell off some lots to pay back the purchase price and expenses for subdivision design, site improvements such as underground utilities and possibly a private shared driveway if there were rear lots, and financing costs.

Our goal was twofold, make a profit on the lot sales plus obtain the best lot at no cost on which to build our colonial home.

My wife was skeptical, saying no one without a lot of money can do it, and you would have to be either a home builder or developer with years of experience. I eventually convinced her it was feasible based upon informal conversations with the developer clients of my employer and hearing how most began their first subdivision development businesses, starting small scale.

Most of them had started as small contractors with just a dump truck and backhoe, grew that into a good size site contractor business, then as a sideline began buying a lot or two from large developers they worked for, building homes on speculation, and eventually buying land tracts for subdivisions of their own.

What they lacked was significant knowledge about the entire subdivision process other than finding a land tract through a realtor and hiring consultants to subdivide it.

So, my wife came around to it being possible for us to do it, by using my subdivision design experience, eliminating the intermediary steps that the developers had gone through, and that our savings could be sufficient for a down payment if we located a small enough tract of land offered with seller financing.

With that conclusion we began to look for that property. And yes, it was possible, we found that property.

## OUR FIRST SUBDIVISION

In looking for that small land tract we used every method we could think of, multiple real estate agencies (no internet then), community board postings such as in coffee shops, inquiring of the Guilford Assessor and Town Clerk if anyone had mentioned they were thinking of selling a land tract, driving every town road with light or no development looking for vacant land with a "For Sale" sign, and also the classified ads of the local newspaper. And bingo, after five months of using all the above methods, a classified ad in the local newspaper brought success.

It was a 13-acre parcel of Guilford woodland with variable terrain, frontage on a quiet town road and had a 50-foot width access strip from the end of pavement of what had become a permanent cul-de-sac road in the adjoining subdivision. The rear boundary of the property was the Neck River, its centerline being the town line between the towns of Guilford and Madison, with the Madison side being State Forest, very private.

We had a verbal agreement with the owner immediately after we walked the property and a signed contract within the week. The property owner financed our purchase with us making a 15% down payment.

Within four plus months the subdivision was designed, had received subdivision and inland wetlands approvals by the Guilford municipal regulatory agencies, and we were installing a rolled gravel common driveway from the cul-de-sac with underground utilities to serve the two rear lots to be offered for sale, and our future homesite lot.

The subdivision consisted of five lots of which we planned (needed) to sell four, the two one acre lots fronting on the quiet town road, two interior (rear) lots of two acres each, to be accessed by a common private driveway extended from the adjoining cul-de-sac road which also served the seven acre lot at the rear of the property we were keeping for our home.

We sold all four lots to a local custom home builder, beginning with the two lots fronting on the quiet town road two months after we purchased the property, and several months later the two rear lots while the common driveway was under construction. We paid off the owner's mortgage eight or nine months after our purchase, and got back our down payment, subdivision design expenses, driveway, and utility installation costs, realizing a nice profit plus our seven-acre lot, a highly successful first subdivision. It was our initial major jump in personal wealth.

Personal plans change, and four years later we divided our seven-acre lot into two lots, selling each lot for double what we paid for the entire 13 acres. Land values had strong growth as homesites were in demand.

The sale funded our next subdivision of 34 acres in an area of Guilford with larger minimum lot area requirements, we only created a total of 4 lots, with 3 of the lots of 2-acre size to be sold to recover our purchase price and all development expenses, and with us keeping a 28-acre estate sized lot on which to build our personal home.

It was followed in a couple of years with us buying the adjoining property of 51 acres, subdividing it into 13 lots, and later in its development obtaining approval to excavate a 900 foot long 4 ½ acre groundwater pond, selling its earth materials for $150,000 (early

1980's dollars) to the excavation contractor who also excavated the pond without cost, significantly increasing the value of the 4 lots which fronted on the pond.

Other subdivisions followed over the years, all of which made us very nice financial returns.

## YOU CAN DO IT TOO – LET THIS BOOK GUIDE YOU

So, whether you presently own land which you plan on being your only subdivision, or you are planning to create a new career as a subdivision developer, the goal for both situations is to maximize the financial potential of each project and complete it as quickly as possible to minimize risk.

So, for you to have success as a developer, whether of a single subdivision or of multiple subdivisions,

I offer you my decades of expertise in both the designing of, and developing of, highly successful residential subdivisions. To gain access to my valuable expertise you only need to take one action, continue reading my book.

This book is the key resource for you to become a successful developer of subdivisions. Everything you need to understand on how to be a successful subdivision developer is provided in my extensive advisory information

### WHAT'S YOUR NEXT STEP?

I recommend focusing on reading the chapters and individual chapter topics which I have asterisked **(*)** as they discuss the most important skills you will need to begin finding and developing your first subdivision. Focus on a property not requiring a proposed road and you will find your first project to be both easy and of minimal cost to purchase and develop. Do so and you are off to becoming a successful developer.

## BEGIN PART-TIME AND KEEP YOUR JOB AND INCOME

You will find that you can begin the initial step of searching for a suitable property without negatively affecting your present job and income. There is sufficient time to look for property on weekends and after work, and its much less time consuming now with real estate listings available on real estate agency's websites versus when I started, no internet.

By the way, all the subdivisions I developed for the first 20 plus years were done while I was a full-time employee of my consultant employer's and subsequently after opening my own consultant practice designing subdivision for developers.

So, get moving reading my book and move on to success!

**PLEASE NOTE:** Throughout this book's content you will only find reference to municipal and state agencies as regulators for approval of a subdivision development, not counties. This is because though Connecticut has counties, they have no regulatory involvement. As many states counties have regulatory authority for approving subdivisions, when municipality is mentioned consider it to also include county regulation.

# CHAPTER 1

## SEEKING A PROPERTY

### OVERVIEW

The topics covered in this chapter are key to understanding whether to, or whether not to consider a specific property to subdivide, methods to use to locate a suitable property, an initial estimation of whether the property upon development is likely to be profitable, and initial, a preliminary due diligence to determine if there are any significant problems with the property.

## INVENTORY OF COMPETITOR SUBDIVISIONS

Prior to beginning a search for a prospective property to develop, such as, in a specific area of a municipality, the municipality in its entirety, or any other defined geographic area, the first and most important step that you must take is to determine the status of subdivision activity in your geographic area of interest.

To determine if an opportunity exists for you to develop a subdivision start by driving around your geographic area of interest looking at where subdivisions are under development and those completed in the past several years.

A reliable resource for understanding whether you should consider developing in a specific area is to meet with the municipal land use staff. Your ability to determine the feasibility of developing a successful subdivision may be significantly influenced by the information they possess.

Most importantly you need to create a subdivision reference base, an inventory of the development status of all subdivisions in your area of interest, identifying where your competitors are or have developed. Ask the land use staff for a break down by subdivision as follows:

**First – An Inventory of Subdivisions, Including Infrastructure Installation Status:**

A.) Infrastructure Completed
B.) Infrastructure Being Installed
C.) No Infrastructure Commenced
D.) Developers Seeking Subdivision Application Approval
E.) Anticipated Subdivision Application Submittals
F.) Preliminary Subdivision Discussion with Land Use Staff
G.) Served by Public Water System?
H.) Served by Public Sewer System?

**Second – Inventory of Each Subdivisions Lot Status:**

A.) Total Lots
B.) Sold or Remaining Lots (Realtors may be of help)

**Third – Inventory Each Subdivisions Home Construction Status – Building Department**

A.) Issued Certificates of Occupancy
B.) Houses Under Construction
C.) Issued Building Permits, Construction Not Begun
D.) Building Permit Applications Submitted for Approval

**Fourth – Municipal Land Records – Town Clerk or Your Realtor**

A.) Sale Prices of Lots
B.) Sale Prices of House/Lot Packages

**Fifth – Other Info of Your Realtor**

A.) Asking Versus Sale Price Ratio
B.) Opinion on market condition, buyer traffic, availability of financing, desirability of a subdivision.

Note the dates of all the above so you can create a flow chart calendar to understand over time the increase / decrease in lots, the market absorption rate, and selling prices as to stable, increasing, or decreasing.

Now you have the necessary data to determine if you should or should not seek a property to develop in your area of interest. Keep in mind your estimated date when your subdivision lots can be sold or built upon, also estimate for that date your competitor's remaining lot inventory and status of infrastructure construction.

# FINDING YOUR PROPERTY TO SUBDIVIDE

## OVERVIEW

The three primary sources developers use to find property:

A.) Realtors
B.) For Sale by Owner
C.) Directly approaching owners

*A possible fourth source is estate attorneys. Often receptive to a direct sale as it negates paying a realtor's commission.*

There are other less common sources for finding property which will be covered shortly. However, whatever the source all properties fall into one of two risk categories dependent upon the degree of due diligence investigation possible.

The opportunity to examine a property is known as, Due Diligence. It is a most critical step in evaluating a property to determine if it is a suitable for your purchase, or if you should pass on it, do not jump on a property without understanding what, if any weaknesses it has. This investigation reduces the likelihood of discovering an unfavorable issue with the property after purchase.

**Note:** I recommend avoiding property when first beginning as a developer that will require installing a public water or sewer system or city gas, as they all can add significantly to development costs.

**Examination Category – Adequate or Limited Due Diligence**
Based upon the extent to which a property can have a due diligence investigation, each property type is classified as follows:

**Due Diligence – Adequate Examination:**

A.) Realtor listings, both MLS and exclusive *1
B.) Private Owner Solicitation*2
C.) For Sale by Owner – Sign on property, internet, or classified ads
D.) Specialized realtors and publications marketing horse farms, farms, ranches, etc.
E.) Non-profit organizations divesting property, such as summer camps
F.) Surplus private water company property
G.) Investment entities divesting a property

**1 A real estate agent who acquires a land listing may attempt to inform only developer/builders where a relationship exists in the period before the listing becomes active* *so as to obtain both sides of the sale and more significantly, an agreement that said agent will be given the listing of the subdivision.*

**2 To avoid Realtor control, the direct approach to owners of land may prove the most successful.*

**Due Diligence – Limited or No Examination (See Note 1):**

A.) Auctions
B.) Tax sales (See Note 2)
C.) Foreclosures
D.) Government seizures
E.) Surplus government property (typically State or County)

***NOTE 1:*** *Some or all, of the preceding may present one or more issues including a greater possibility of having an undisclosed environmental issue which Buyer will likely become financially responsible to resolve.*

***NOTE 2:*** *Tax sales/auctions generally are held after several years of non-payment of taxes, if you review and generate a list of property's with several years of unpaid taxes but not yet ripe for a tax sale/auction, consider approaching the owner with an offer to purchase.*

**CAUTION:** If considering purchase of a partially completed subdivision, or an approved subdivision which never commenced infrastructure construction, see, Chapter 14, Construction Infrastructure – Commencement and Completion Deadlines, and "Chapter 17, Warnings – Subdivision Declared Null and Void.

**Finally**. Do not be afraid to pass up on initial properties you find by justifying that a problem isn't all that bad, stick to the criteria you have set, you will find many more properties to consider, patience pays.

**SO, WHAT NOW? WELL, READ ON.**

**Finding a Realtor**.

Vacant land tracts are seldom the strong point of most real estate agents I have met. Most focus on homes, new and existing, a few are informed about individual building lots, while those with expertise in finding and listing developable land tracts are not that common.

Two methods to find a real estate agent knowledgeable in land tracts:

A.) An attorney whose practice represents subdivision developers

B.) The advertising signage at a subdivision's entrance, typically a realtor is listed on it, as developers generally list the subdivision with the agent who found it, contact the agent.

However, be aware that when you locate an agent who is in the "very small circle" of agents capable of finding and then listing developable land tracts, it is highly likely that they have an existing business relationship with one or more developers. These developers will almost always be informed of the listing before the listing reaches MLS, and the property may be under contract before the wider market has an opportunity to participate.

So, what to do Realtor wise? Discuss with those qualified land agents you have located, that you are starting out in the subdivision development business, that you recognize they have long term developer relationships. Sound them out if they would contact you if a land tract is not of interest to their developer clientele, and by given the opportunity to make an offer, if accepted, the listings for lot sales will be theirs.

If you aren't able to obtain a commitment from an agent connected to land development, then you are left with choosing a established general real estate agent to advise you of any MLS land listings and stress they will get the listing on lots.

**For Sale by Owner.**

Owners of land tracts may post For Sale signs on the property, place a classified ad in the local newspaper, or today on the internet. The first land tract that I personally purchased was from an owner with an ad in the classified ads of the local newspaper. The success of that small subdivision enabled me to develop subdivisions individually and in partnership for over 30 years.

**Directly Approaching Landowners.**

This method can be the most successful, but it takes time to identify properties of interest and frequently perseverance in obtaining a meeting with the property owner. I recommend initially contacting an owner by way of a professional business letter sent by mail. A phone call is too informal and could be viewed as a scam. Showing up unannounced at the front door is such a no, no.

When you get the opportunity to meet the owner, have a concise presentation and why the property's sale to you, will provide a greater benefit to the owner (the most obvious is no real estate sales commission).

**Two Sources to Find Landowners**.

**Tax Maps**. At the municipal or county Assessors' Office review the tax maps for parcels of land of the size, shape, and road frontage you are seeking. Each property will have a unique identifier from which the Assessors indexes will provide the owners name, address, etc.

**The Grand List.** Useful if parcel area is the sole initial search criteria. It will also provide the name of the owner, property address (some municipalities do not assign addresses to vacant land but reference the tax map identifier) and the owner mailing address.

Once you have identified potential land tracts from the Tax Maps, if the municipality or county have topographic maps and/or wetlands mapping, determine if either, or both negatively impact a property as to its potential for subdivision development. This process can eliminate investing time on a land tract with limited development potential.

## THE AMERICAN WEST

Just before submitting my book for publication, I felt that I needed to say something regarding the double whammy much of the West has been experiencing, massive wildfires and severe long-term drought.

Sitting back here on the East coast I want to make it clear that my comments are not professionally based but from observation of the national news on television and the internet.

I suspect that regulatory agencies for subdivision development are probably behind the curve as to modifying or creating regulations and standards to meet these challenges to living and developing in areas of the West. Throw in the slower bureaucracy of the federal agencies and you are left with questions as to whether and where development is still viable.

I think you should be monitoring closely the possibility that moratoriums could be placed on swathes of land throughout western states. Possibly it may have already begun.

These threats unfortunately will apparently be with us for decades, there is no magic bullet for a quick reversal. So, be careful in considering an offer to purchase a property, you may want to consult with professionals in the field of long-term forecasting of environmental issues.

Your attorney should discuss with you appropriate contract clauses related to these climate issues to permit you to extract yourself from an agreement to purchase if these conditions arise or worsen in your area before a scheduled closing. Be prudent and good luck.

# ESTIMATION OF SUBDIVISION PROFITABILITY

## OVERVIEW

So, you have now found a property of interest. It may be in an area where there are existing homes or possibly in proximity to where other subdivisions are being developed attracting buyer interest, the big question now is will it be a profitable subdivision.

Determination of the estimated profitability **(P)** of a property is dependent upon two key components, the estimated market value **(MV)** of the subdivision when completed, less its acquisition and estimated development expenses **(E)**. So, Profitability: **P = MV – E.**

If specific technical information on the property exists, such as, a property survey map, terrain topography, and wetlands mapping, then from a compilation of them, a conceptual subdivision layout can be created, providing:

A.) A lot yield of the property which then provides the basis for determining the estimated market value of the completed subdivision

B.) The ability for estimation of the subdivision infrastructure improvements and costs

C.) The gross profit of the subdivision can then be estimated by deducting from the estimated market value, the estimated infrastructure improvement costs.

If some or all the above property information does not exist (often likely) then alternative information must be sought. Potential sources are: the Assessors tax maps in lieu of a property survey map; USGS quadrangle topographic maps; the municipalities official map of inland wetlands, to create a compilation plan of the property, the basis for a conceptual subdivision layout.

The less specific information is about a property, consider taking a more conservative approach on estimation of both market value (lower) and development costs (higher), this will decrease the likelihood of committing to a property that may disappoint as to its profitability.

## ANALYSIS and DETERMINATION

### Estimated Market Value (MV)

### Competitor's Lot Sales

If there are subdivisions in proximity with sold lots and/or lots for sale, it is a useful reference in developing your market valuation.

### Competitor's Home/Lot Sales

For subdivision developers building homes, often the development of the subdivision lots and the homebuilding are legally separate business entities, and the lots "sold" by the development entity to the homebuilding entity, raises the question of whether the lot "sold price" was an arms-length sale or was purposedly a higher or lower price than fair market value for internal business purposes.

### Market Value Per Desired Profitability, MV = P+E

In a strong real estate market developers may take the approach that the profit (P) they seek plus its estimated development expenses I equals the market value (MV) of the completed subdivision.

### Subdivision Development Expenses, E:

#### Property Acquisition

A.) Purchase price to be adjusted for any increase or decrease in the number of approved lots versus the number of lots cited in the contract

B.) Closing adjustments.

#### Development Expenses

A.) Subdivision design and associated consultant fees

B.) Regulatory agencies application fees and consultant presentation fees

C.) Financing costs

D.) Property taxes

E.) Liability insurance

F.) Installation of infrastructure improvements (i.e., roads, utilities, etc.)

G.) Expenses for unexpected work and materials price increases

H.) Surveying and engineering – infrastructure installation and post installation as-builts

I.) Miscellaneous expenses

J.) Sales commissions

K.) Site maintenance

L.) Legal

### Project Profitability Estimation

The Estimated Market Value from one of the above methods less Project Development Expenses yields the best estimation of the profitability of a property and whether it is prudent to proceed with a purchase offer.

**To Consider When Applicable**

If the municipality where you propose to develop, either assesses impact fees on new subdivisions, and/or imposes a significant increase in property taxes upon approval of a subdivision, make sure to include them in development expenses.

Also, if you eventually move into building the homes in your subdivision, and lots are not to be served by either a public water supply and/or sewer system, but instead by individual wells and/or subsurface sewage disposal systems on each lot, include their cost in your estimate of infrastructure improvements costs.

As profitability estimation is dependent on as precise as possible estimation of development expenses, they should be delegated to your engineer or construction estimator consultant, financing costs to your banker or accountant, and anticipated lot values at the anticipated time when available for sale, to an appraiser and/or realtor with established record of marketing subdivisions.

## PRELIMINARY DUE DILIGENCE PRIOR TO CONTRACT SUBMITTAL

### OVERVIEW

There are several necessary investigatory steps you must pursue to determine if the property is a good venture before submitting an offer to purchase the property, they follow below.

However, some of the following you may decide to postpone because of time limitations to submit an offer to beat out potential competitors, until you have a signed contract, then performing them during the contract due diligence period.

### EVALUATIONS

### QUESTIONS OF SELLER

The Seller Listing Agreement and any required associated documents may not disclose certain information that is important to you in deciding whether to make an offer to purchase, so ask the seller.

A.) Is there more than one owner? If yes, all must sign a sale agreement unless one owner has been authorized to act on behalf of all owners, if so, request the authorization document.

B.) Is the property subject to an Option to Purchase or a Right of First Refusal? If yes, status?
C.) Existing Lease? If yes, written or verbal? Purpose? Expiration Date?
D.) Encroachments? By an adjoining property? By Seller upon adjoiner?
E.) A governmental body or a non-profit organization wanting to acquire the property?
F.) Subject to Liens or a Lis Pendens?
G.) Are property taxes paid current?
H.) Has there ever been an Adverse Possession claim lawsuit? If yes, the outcome?
I.) Do you have a property survey map not recorded in the land records? Are boundary lines in dispute? Are any boundaries unknown to you?
J.) Is a boundary line agreement in discussion, agreed upon, or ready for recordation?
K.) Are you aware of any environmental violation? If yes, specifics.
L.) Is the property collateral for a mortgage? Balance due? Is it current? Date term ends? Lender?

**PROPERTY INSPECTION**

A.) Walk the property thoroughly, both its perimeter and interior.
B.) Does property appear to have sufficient developable area?
C.) Extent and location of unsuitable land such as, ledge, wetlands, water bodies.
D.) Is there suitable access for subdivision road(s) and driveways from an improved public road?
E.) Are utilities available at the property, if not, distance to them?
F.) Potentially hazardous areas: cliffs; extremely steep slopes; water body with steep slope below surface
G.) Any visible, potential hazardous materials or debris?
H.) Is there a high-tension electric transmission line or unused easement upon property?
I.) Is there a gas transmission pipeline or unused easement upon property?
J.) Are there nonresidential facilities adjoining or in proximity to property?

**I recommend thar you have a land surveyor or engineer with you on your first property inspection.**

**EXAMINATION OF PUBLIC RECORDS**

**<u>Town Clerks Office</u>**

**Deed of Property:**

A.) Type of Deed: Warranty; Quit-Claim; Executor; etc., obtain copies

B.) Confirm: Seller is owner; Cite of property area; Cite of a property survey map; If yes, is it recorded in the land records, if not, obtain a copy from the land surveyor.

**Third Party Rights:**

A.) Does the deed indicate any existing rights possessed by others?
B.) Does a third party have the ability to extend a right to others?

**Easements:**

A.) Pass and repass
B.) Drainage
C.) Utilities
D.) Communication tower

**Leases:**

A.) Right of use
B.) Mineral Extraction
C.) Water rights – surface and subsurface

**Liens / Notices / Foreclosure:**

A.) Tax Liens – Municipal, County, State, Federal, and Mechanics Lien (Service Provider)
B.) Notice of Lis Pendens (notice of a filed lawsuit)
C.) Foreclosure – Status of

## Assessor's Office

A.) Tax Map
B.) Property records
C.) Classification of property
D.) Valuation of property

## Planning and/or Zoning or Land Use Office

A.) Confirm zone of property and immediately adjoining properties
B.) Obtain copies of all regulations pertinent to subdividing land: Zoning, Subdivision, Plan of Development, Road Ordinance, and any other regulations pertinent to subdivisions

C.) Inspect FEMA maps to determine if a property is within a flood zone(s), and its zone(s)

## Inland Wetland or Environmental Office

A.) Official Wetlands Map
B.) List of regulated activities
C.) List of exempt or of-right activities in wetlands

## QUESTIONS OF REGULATORY AGENCIES STAFF

## Planning and/or Zoning Office or Land Use Office

### Moratoriums

If any moratorium is applicable to subdivision applications or another land use agency application or connection to municipal sewage or water systems (if required to serve property) please identify.

A.) Is a moratorium in effect? What for? When ending?
B.) Any approved moratorium with a pending start date? What for? When ending?
C.) Is a moratorium awaiting action on a motion to adopt? What For? For how long?
D.) Is a moratorium under discussion or consideration? What for?

### Zoning

A.) Existence of, or proposed non-residential zone adjacent to your property of interes
B.) Inquiries as to perspective of commission on a zone changet

### Regulations or Standards – Proposed Revisions:

A.) Zoning Districts or Regulations
B.) Subdivision Regulations
C.) Wetlands – Inland and Tidal Regulations
D.) Plan of Development
E.) Environmental or Conservation Regulations
F.) Health Department standards – subsurface sewage disposal systems
G.) Road Ordinance Design Standards

If the above preliminary property investigations determine conditions or facts not acceptable to you, either an offer to purchase should not be submitted, or the conditions or facts of concern should be specified in your offer to purchase as subject to further investigation to your satisfaction.

# CHAPTER 2

## PLANNING AND MODERATING DEVELOPMENT COSTS

### OVERVIEW

The planning and financial steps to subdivide property successfully are critical.

**Planning**: Decreases the potential for lower lot yield and more extensive infrastructure construction

**Financial:** Unless you have substantial personal funds, to purchase, design, develop, and pay maintenance, liability insurance, property taxes and other such expenses, borrowing will be necessary until sales of lots or homes have paid down expenses.

**However:** If you are not flush with cash, be aware of an alternative method to help finance subdivisions.

## A PROPERTY CAN HELP PAY ITS DEVELOPMENT COSTS

**There are four principle financial components to most subdivisions:**

A.) Land acquisition
B.) Subdivision design
C.) Infrastructure construction (if applicable)
D.) Bonding

To pay the above, developers typically on a project-by-project basis, either possess all, or a sufficient percentage of the monies needed, or have a strong credit history to borrow from a lender.

**Land is purchased by one of the following methods:**

A.) Developer possesses sufficient funds to purchase it outright
B.) Developer has partial purchase funds, and the ability to obtain financing of the balance

C.) A seller willing to finance all, or a portion of the purchase price (great, however I recommend avoiding direct seller participation unless you want to surrender a portion of the profit).

D.) Option To Purchase (I recommend only if you and the seller wish to postpone purchase for a number of years, I see it as being of no of use to a first time developer).

Upon obtaining ownership or control of a property through a signed, purchase/sale agreement, you have the potential to secure some or all the financing necessary for its development by using the land as collateral.

If borrowing is necessary, it can be controlled by developing the subdivision by sections, this will spread the expenses for subdivision design, infrastructure installation and bonding amongst each section.

For an individual's first subdivision, I would recommend that it be a small property with significant road frontage and no need for internal road infrastructure. It could have some lots to the rear lots fronting on the street, accessed by either individual or shared driveways, very minimal development cost.

If you also focus on property where no public water or sewage systems exist, and there is no requirement to extend them to the subdivision, the lots will instead be served by individual wells and subsurface sewage disposal systems for which the installation and expense will be the responsibility of the lot purchaser.

A property meeting these criteria eliminates a significant amount of expense, then when you are financially established by developing your first subdivision, you can undertake larger projects with road infrastructure.

Following are several ways irrespective of the method of purchase to reduce development expenses.

## SPLIT AS-OF-RIGHT

Another practical way to reduce development expenses and additionally provide quicker cash flow is a method available per Connecticut General Statutes, which I used whenever the property met its criteria. Commonly referred to as, **"a first split"** or **"split as-of-right,"** check if your State Statutes permit it.

This method is available for a property that has not had any land deeded out that met the zoning standards for a conforming lot, subsequent to the adoption of subdivision regulations by the municipality

If that condition is met, one lot conforming to the current zoning standards may be created and separated from the property exempt from the requirement of being created by the subdivision process. This allows such a lot to be immediately sold or built upon.

This method reduces some of the development expenses, bonding, and open space area when subdividing the remainder of the property, providing cash from the lot sale to help fund the development expenses of the subdivision.

## DEVELOPMENT BY SECTIONS = COST CONTROL

### OVERVIEW

Whether your subdivision begins with a **"split-by-right,"** or not, subdividing the entire property as a single application may not be the be best business decision, especially for your first subdivision.

**Why? Because then you have expenses for:**

A.) Final design of the entire subdivision
B.) Installing all subdivision infrastructure improvements
C.) Posting a performance bond for all subdivision infrastructure improvements
D.) Financing of the entire subdivision and its interest payments
E.) Property taxes for all, instead of for a portion of the lots

Also, if during your sales phase, the absorption rate for new subdivision homes or lots softens, project income will decrease but interest payments for any financing, and property taxes remain constant.

Clients of my consultant practice with large subdivisions who had installed all infrastructure improvements at once, sometimes found themselves in a tight financial situation because of market conditions, sectional subdividing would have moderated the impact. Those clients to which this happened switched to sectional subdivisions in future large projects. However, sectional subdividing is beneficial to all size subdivisions.

During your search for a property verify if the municipalities subdivision regulations allow for sectional subdividing. The larger your subdivision, the more important it is to have this option available.

**Sectional subdividing postpones portions of the following expenses:**

A.) Site infrastructure installation (i.e., the big cost item being roads)
B.) Financing interest payments
C.) Subdivision application fees (when fees based per lot)
D.) Performance bonding

E.) Consultant design fees
F.) Property tax increases for approved/improved lots

Effective sectional subdividing of a property does require that certain investigations be done for the entire property so the ideal lot and road layout can be determined for the entire subdivision. Only the first section is then finalized for the initial application to subdivide.

**Necessary technical services for the entire property:**

A.) Property (Boundary) survey and map
B.) Investigation for the presence or not, of wetlands, inland and/or tidal
C.) The location and mapping of any wetlands
D.) Application presentation for wetlands boundary approval and application fee
E.) Topography of the property as either required per subdivision regulations or by your project engineer for road, drainage, and other design requirements
F.) For non-public sewer served subdivisions, soils investigation for individual on-site sewage disposal systems.

If wetlands are present, they should be located and a boundary map for the entire property prepared as part of the initial work, then submitted for approval as the official boundary of the property by the Inland Wetlands Commission.

The above steps are critical to avoid the possibility for significant subdivision layout design changes due to unexpected terrain situations, such as wetlands in a future section.

Following the above suggested steps will allow for the preparation of an overall preliminary subdivision layout, the basis for determining section boundaries.

As each section is next to be developed, its final design plans can be prepared, and a subdivision application submitted to the Planning and Zoning Commission for action. If there also is proposed construction in inland wetlands, a regulated activity application must be submitted to the Inland Wetlands Commission for action.

Subsequent sectional subdivision applications will eventually subdivide the entire property.

If a municipality's regulations do not include sectional subdividing, but also does not specifically prohibit it, and if time permits in your schedule, consider discussing informally with the Planning and Zoning Commission their attitude towards modifying their regulations to adopt them.

Most lenders require the entire subdivision property as collateral for loans, possibly even when you subdivide by sections, try to find a lender that will limit collateral for a loan on a sectional basis.

A method that could eliminate a lenders ability to collateralize the entire property in a sectional development is by purchasing a section at a time from the Seller, as long as you have an option to purchase the remaining property on a sectional basis. This may also be beneficial to the Seller with respect to their financial planning goals and/or tax situation.

## METHODS TO REDUCE DEVELOPMENT COSTS

### OVERVIEW

Physical assets existing on a property may have the potential to reduce development costs. An inspection of the property to inventory any useful assets is your first step.

### TYPICAL PHYSICAL ASSETS:

**Woodland properties:**

A.) Trees with a diameter to yield dimensional timber
B.) High value furniture grade trees, i.e., walnut
C.) Trees suitable for firewood or pallet construction.

The value of the above varies, but all offer the possibility that the development costs of clearing a road right-of-way, shared driveways, and home sites can be offset or even turn a profit by a forestry products firms purchase of this resource.

**Topsoil.** If fields have topsoil with a depth exceeding the depth criteria of topsoil needed to restore disturbed areas post construction, sell the surplus, it is in demand and has value.

**Fieldstone walls.** Used for architectural purposes, fireplaces, foundations above grade, privacy walls.

**Pond creation:**

A.) Excavated soils suitable for construction, use on-site and/or sale
B.) Lots with frontage/view of pond, adds value to these lots
C.) If fire protection is required and a public water supply is not available, a pond may be less expensive than a fire water tank installation plus it has aesthetic appeal.

**Blasted ledge – crushed:**

A.) Road construction
B.) Rip rap for storm water drainage discharge structures
C.) Bedding for driveways and cellar floors.

### STORM WATER MANAGEMENT:

If internal roads are proposed, storm water drainage by sheet flow off the edges of the road if permitted by regulations, eliminates all or much of the typical storm water drainage system expense.

## FINANCING THE SUBDIVISION

Using one or all of the preceding topics; "A Property Can Help Pay Its Subdivision Costs"; "Split-As-Of-Right"; "Development By Sections = Cost Control"; and "Methods To Reduce Development Costs", and you find that some financing is necessary, there are traditional sources and not so traditional sources of financing.

Among the traditional financing sources are: commercial banks; commercial mortgage brokers; partners of yours in other businesses; family members; personal friends; and insurance companies, though they likely are only interested in large projects; the seller of the property; and homebuilders who see it as a way to be the dominant or exclusive builder for your subdivision.

For the less traditional financing sources: attorneys and realtors who put together small investment groups from their clients; hard money lenders, but be careful as they are expensive and offer little or no leeway with regards to the terms of the loan; owners of large heavy equipment firms which lease construction equipment to local builders and contractors; owners of wholesale lumber and building supply companies to the local construction and building industry, and I'm sure many others.

With regard to any of the above providing financing, you may want to avoid any offer tying financing to their becoming a partner in the subdivision, unless you find it acceptable to give up some of your future profit.

## AVOIDING THE PITFALL OF NOT PLANNING

### OVERVIEW

During my professional years as a Connecticut consultant designing residential subdivisions there were several clients who were generational owners of large land tracts, former farms from Connecticut's fading farming days.

Many of these clients wanted to subdivide a few lots out of the farm to gift them to their children to build their homes. As no money was to be received by the parents, they wanted to spend as little money as possible to create the lots.

This often caused a problem when a more extensive subdivision of the farm was proposed in later years.

Individuals in the business of subdividing land understand that a thorough investigation of the property by consultants is the key element in creating a subdivision layout that maximizes lot yield and minimizes infrastructure.

To realize this outcome, there is only one solution, the expenditure of money, not what these owners wanted.

So, many family farms in creating lots for the kids with marginal money available meant no overall property planning, and to top it off, children were often permitted to select their lot locations wherever they choose.

Additionally, lots often had irregular shapes, and/or exceptionally large areas.

These scattered lots often became an issue when in later years the parents or their heirs (the children) decided to subdivide a major portion of, or the entirety of the farm, then the lack of initial planning often became obvious.

This often resulted in a lower total lot yield both due to the randomness of the lots and unknown terrain and wetlands constraints not having been earlier investigated. Road locations were often not able to fully take advantage of the ideal locations for roads due to the afore mentioned lack of planning, often resulting in both higher development costs and lower profit for the owners.

**How To Avoid This Outcome**

A.) Retain a land surveyor to begin the technical work:
- 1.) Property (Boundary) survey map
- 2.) Wetlands: inspection, location, a boundary map, and regulatory approval as the official boundary
- 3.) Terrain topography mapping (if required)

B.) Conceptual subdivision lot and road plan for entire farm

C.) Sell a lot or two to a non-family member to generate the funds for proper consultant planning

D.) Guide children's lot locations to minimize or eliminate negative impact on lot yield.

# CHAPTER 3

## PURCHASE CONTRACT

### OVERVIEW

My experience in Connecticut with real estate Purchase/Sale Agreements (a.k.a. the "Contract") provided through realtor associations, is that they are structured for making a purchase offer for a home and are inadequate for making an offer to purchase a land tract intended for a subdivision.

Your offer to purchase should be developed in consultation with an attorney specializing in land use and its development. Avoid using an attorney whose practice and experience is house closings.

This consultation is particularly important so that your offer has no omissions that could negatively affect your project. Your contract needs to protect you in the matters unique to subdividing property, revising a signed purchase/sale agreement for an unforeseen situation may not be acceptable to the Seller.

Experienced land development attorneys should have a Purchase/Sale Agreement crafted specifically for the purpose of a land purchase for subdivision development. Such attorney crafted contracts provide substantial Developer (Buyer) protection, however I found in my personal and partnership land development purchases, that even these contracts lacked some particularly important Developer protections.

This chapter identifies certain clauses I recommend be included in the Conditions section of the Purchase/Sale Agreement.

A comment about options. They are suitable for established developers who are well funded, not individuals new to development. Why? Options are for the possible purchase of a property by a future date, not immediately. They also have the risk that you lose the option money when the option is not closed prior to its termination date.

## CONTRACT CONDITIONS (CONTINGENCIES):

A.) Offered Purchase Price. Specify that it is to be adjusted if the number of approved, subdivision lots is different than the number of lots cited with respect to the offered purchase price. The purchase price being adjusted up or down by a specified dollar amount for each lot greater or lesser than the number of lots cited in your offer of purchase. (This protects both parties from a fixed purchase price being unfavorable for one party if the approved lots are dissimilar to the number specified in the contract. Lenders also may require this condition for a loan).

B.) Buyer Due Diligence Investigations. You and the seller must agree on the length of time for due diligence, however it is important that the length of time matches as closely as possible the recommendations of your technical consultants, as they are the ones performing the investigations. Advise your attorney that the due diligence condition also includes the phrase, "including any unexpected investigation(s) determined to be necessary by buyer consultants."

C.) All surveys, maps, plans, reports, studies, and documents performed on behalf of the buyer and at buyer expense is the sole property of the buyer.

D.) Closing Date. It shall be extended if any of the following occurs:

1.) Until the termination of the statutory period for any party to file an appeal with Superior Court of an approval of subdivision obtained by the applicant.

2.) Denial of plaintiff's appeal of subdivision approval by Superior Court.

3.) Denial of plaintiff's appeal to Superior Court of its denial, or the end of the deadline to appeal said denial.

3.) Denial of plaintiff's appeal by the Appellate Court of Superior Court's denial, or the end of the deadline to appeal said denial.

4.) Denial of plaintiff's appeal to Appellate Court of its denial, or the end of the deadline to appeal said denial.

5.) Refusal by the Supreme Court of plaintiff's petition for the court to hear an appeal of the Appellate Court's denial, or denial by the Supreme Court of plaintiff's appeal of the Appellate Court denial.

E.) No seller reservation of, granting of, or sale of, post seller signing of Purchase/ Sale Agreement of any mineral, water, or other natural resource rights.

F.) Seller to cease or not initiate activities in violation of municipal ordinances and regulatory agencies regulations, or the as-is condition of the property.

G.) Buyer has right to act on behalf of the seller in response to, including initiating legal action against:

1.) Proposed change of zone

2.) Proposed change of zoning, planning, wetlands, conservation, road, and storm drainage standards, public health standards for subsurface sewage disposal systems, and any other land use and development regulations, standards, or ordinances.

3.) Eminent domain
4.) Proposed taking for widening of an existing road right-of-way
5.) Adverse possession claim
6.) Encroachment by adjoining property owner(s)
7.) Proposed moratorium(s) for:
  A.) Public sewage hook-up or extension
  B.) Public water system hook-up or extension
  C.) Soils testing for individual lot on-site or community subsurface sewage disposal systems
  D.) Application submission for subdivision of property

H.) Buyer right to post no trespassing signage upon the property.
I.) Buyer right to post signage announcing future subdivision (if permitted by regulations).
J.) Buyer right to initiate legal action for an application denial or unfavorable condition(s) of approval.
K.) Purchase/Sale Agreement, automatic extension of the closing date necessitated by:
  1.) Request by a regulatory agency for additional time to consider an application.
  2.) Regulatory commission failure to have a meeting quorum.
  3.) Regulatory commission cancellation of a meeting.
  4.) Regulatory commission awaiting a report by staff, their consultant(s), or by another agency.
  5.) Regulatory commission request for unanticipated work by applicants' consultants.

## BUYER ACCESS TO PROPERTY

If a vacant land tract is posted with a "For Sale by Owner" sign, do not assume this means you should immediately access the property on your own. Call the listed phone number for owner permission and inquire if a map of the property exists and if the owner would walk the property with you to better understand the property.

However, if a vacant land tract is identified for sale with realtor signage, the realtor will have the owner's permission to grant prospects the right to walk the property, generally with the agent, which is preferable as the agent may have specific knowledge about the property not in the listing.

If you don't have your own agent then you have the opportunity to let the agent know the type of property you are seeking and have another set of eyes looking on your behalf.

If the owner has a classified ad in a newspaper or on the internet, the owner can give you verbal permission to access the property, however tell the owner you would appreciate it if the owner would walk it with you to better understand the property. It is also good to develop a personal connection as you may have to convince the owner besides a solid offer, that you are the party it should be sold to.

The Purchase/Sale Agreement must specify as a condition, Buyer and your consultants and agents having the right of access to the property. This is necessary so your consultants can perform your due diligence investigations.

You and your consultants shall have the right of access commencing upon your receipt of the owner signed contract, and this access right shall continue until your closing on the property.

Access rights shall also include regulatory agencies staff, commission members, public utility companies' staff, and a site or excavation contractor and equipment.

Access shall continue post regulatory agency action, whether an approval or denial, if legal action is taken by any third party, yourself (Buyer), or any other regulatory agency.

## SELLER PROHIBITIONS

As the Buyer you should include in your Purchase/Sale Agreement offer specific conditions to preclude actions of the Owner (Seller) unintentional or not, but which could impact negatively on the subdivision process and Buyer future enjoyment of the property.

The conditions are a notice to the owner of the buyer expectations that the owner will not engage in the described activities beginning upon seller signing of the offer, continuing in effect until buyer closes on the property.

**Recommended Contract Conditions of Owner Prohibitions:**

A.) Seller shall not enter upon the property once buyer investigation activities upon the property have begun, without the permission of the buyer (except for a limited area around seller's residence if on the property)

B.) Seller shall not give permission to a third party to access property

C.) Seller shall not grant or extend any leases

D.) Seller shall not initiate contact or interact with any regulatory agency or agency advisory body involved in, or anticipated to be involved in, the processes of acting upon the Buyers subdivision application, or a non-profit organization typically interested in a subdivision's open space, such as but not limited to, a local land preservation trust

E.) Seller shall not interact with any media regarding the development of the property
F.) Seller shall not enter into any boundary line agreement without the consent of the Buyer
G.) Seller shall not grant any easements, right-of-way, or drainage discharge rights
H.) Seller shall not further encumber the property as collateral for loans

## LIABILITY – BUYER AND SELLER

Both the Buyer and Seller have the responsibility to obviously protect their respective interests, but also the other party by having or placing in effect liability insurance coverage.

The buyer shall be responsible for enforcing all buyer agents and contractors having liability insurance coverage. Additionally, if either party performing services for the buyer has employees, Workmen's Compensation coverage shall be in effect.

Your insurance professional should be consulted on the appropriate amount of coverage, and whether the Seller should be named as an insured party on your policy, and vice versa.

Buyer and seller shall provide each other with a copy of their insurance coverage. Buyer and seller insurers shall provide the other party a copy of any notice sent to their insured, such as:

A.) Any change in coverage or named insured
B.) Default by insured
C.) Late or non-payment of premium due
D.) Cancellation of a policy by either the insured or the insurance company
E.) Change in insurer by insured

If there are any third parties with the right of accessing the property or have lease rights, discuss the situation with both your insurer and attorney as to how best to protect yourself from any potential claim arising from their access to the property.

Buyer insurer of your personal residence may be able to include liability coverage of the property as a rider to your homeowner's policy without additional premium. However, if the subdivision has any infrastructure improvements that you must install once construction commences you would need a commercial liability policy.

# CHAPTER 4

## PROFESSIONAL CONSULTANTS

### OVERVIEW

If this is your first time developing a subdivision you need to be aware of the various professions that you will need to hire to prepare the maps, plans, reports, and documents required by regulatory agencies for submittal of, and action on, applications for subdivision, and subsequent to approval construction layout and supervision of installation of infrastructure improvements, and as-builts of the completed infrastructure improvements.

## CONSULTANTS AND SERVICES – REQUIRED

### DESIGN PHASE

**Land Surveyor:**

A.) Boundary (Property) Survey Map
B.) Division Map (if needed)
C.) Topographic Map (contours of property), based upon aerial photography flown specifically for the property, or a statewide flight on behalf of the State, or a field topographic survey of the property, or compiled from existing federal governmental topographic mapping (USGS)
D.) Wetlands Boundary Mapping, inland and/or tidal (when present)
E.) Existing Conditions Plan (a compilation of any combination of the above maps)
F.) Preliminary Lot-Road Layout PlaN
G.) Location of soils testing for subsurface sewage disposal systems (if no public sewage system)
H.) Subdivision Map

**Engineer – Civil/Site:**

A.) Soils investigation and suitability report for subsurface sewage disposal systems (unless to be served by a public sewage sewer system)

B.) Design of subdivision roads and its storm water drainage system

C.) Storm water management analysis of subdivision post development, design of any required on-site detention and/or retention structures, and if necessary, off-site drainage improvements

D.) Detailed design of wetlands crossings (when present) by roads, driveways, and utilities

E.) Site Development Plan of subdivision (may possibly be prepared by the land surveyor)

**Soil Scientist or Other Designated Profession:**

A.) Inspection to determine the presence or not of wetlands, if present, identification of the wetlands soil types, and field delineation of the boundaries for location by a land surveyor

B.) Report of wetlands inspection findings

C.) Remediation recommendations and/or plan to address loss of wetlands post development (if required by wetlands regulations or mandated during consideration of application)

## POST DESIGN PHASE

## BID QUANTITY ESTIMATES, CONSTRUCTION LAYOUT, AND AS-BUILT PLANS

**Land Surveyor:**

A.) Mark construction clearing limits, particularly important for woodland properties

B.) Construction layout of subdivision infrastructure improvements

C.) As-built plan(s) of all completed subdivision infrastructure improvements

**NOTE:** Excludes underground utilities, excepting the above ground components

**Engineer – Civil / Site:**

A.) Infrastructure improvements materials specifications and quantity estimates

B.) Bid document for infrastructure improvements (the non-technical portion should be prepared by your attorney)

C.) Monitoring of installation of subdivision infrastructure improvements as complying with design plans, materials specifications, and proper installation

D.) Progress reports (typically monthly) of installed infrastructure improvements for partial payments to infrastructure contractor (prior to Developer issuing payment concurrence of municipalities inspector, and lenders agent, if any, should first be obtained)

E.) Request letter(s) to municipality for partial reduction of performance bonding for the portion of infrastructure installed, and upon completion of all installation work, release of the remaining bonding

F.) Request of municipality for acceptance of all public infrastructure improvements

**NOTE:** Your contract with the infrastructure contractor selected must be prepared by your attorney

**NOTE:** Request letters noted in 5 and 6 above maybe prepared by yourself, a land surveyor or attorney.

## CONSULTANTS AND SERVICES – AS REQUIRED

Either the regulations of agencies involved in considering subdivision applications or a specific investigation requested by a regulatory agency during the hearing of your application could require you to provide the agency with additional reports, documents, plans, etc., prepared by the appropriate professional consultant, such as:

**Traffic Engineer:**

A.) Traffic study, report, and recommendations (typically if a subdivision road is accessing a state highway or very busy municipal road)

**Civil / Site Engineer:**

A.) Design of by-pass and/or deceleration lane (typically limited to a state highway)

**Environmentalist:**

A.) Impact of development and recommendations for any remediation (may be for services either beyond the professional capabilities of a soil scientist or mandated in lieu of a soil scientist).

B.) A plan depicting specifics of remediation recommendations.

**Archaeologist:**

A.) Regulations may require the evaluation of either all properties or only those known or suspected to contain archaeological sites;

B.) Report including opinion of site importance and recommendation as to whether permanent preservation or just documentation of the site should be required.

**Architect:**

A.) Generally, not required for single family home subdivisions but may be required for certain types of single-family subdivisions such as, cluster or detached accessory apartment;

B.) If required, may be either conceptual rendering for visual presentation or detailed plans.

**Landscape Architect:**

A.) Location plan for street trees with specie(s), size, planting instructions;

B.) Possible selective plantings to screen adjoining properties for privacy concerns;

C.) Subdivision entrance(s) plantings;

D.) Plantings required per regulations for individual lots

E.) Inspection for ancient or rare species trees.

**Land Surveyor:**

A.) Location and mapping of any ancient or rare species trees, and limits of archaeological areas;

B.) Location and mapping of any man-made protected features, such as, fieldstone walls, ruins of old mill and dam sites, foundation remains, and family, colonial, or native cemeteries.

## SELECTING YOUR PROFESSIONAL CONSULTANTS

### OVERVIEW

If this is your first subdivision development you will need to initially locate professionals in these three fields, land surveying, civil or site engineering, and an attorney. They will be the nucleus of your professional consultant team. Some subdivision projects may require other professionals either because investigatory or design work finds them necessary to address an aspect of development or due to being specified in a municipality's regulations or at the request of a regulatory commission or its staff.

## PRUDENT STEPS PRIOR TO LOCATING A PROPERTY

There are activities you need to be involved in before you locate a potential property, especially finding the professional consultants for your subdivision. They are a land surveyor, civil engineer, and attorney.

I recommend that you evaluate several prospective professionals for each area of expertise. Begin your search and evaluation while you are looking for a property, you may locate it sooner than expected and you always need to focus on minimizing non-productive time, a developer's worst enemy as time is money.

As you meet with the various consultants and attorneys during your interviewing process, ask questions, you are not meeting with them only to introduce yourself, this is your due diligence of them individually and of their firms, that is how you will be able to narrow each profession down to choosing the right consultants

## NOW BEGINS THE DETECTIVE WORK

My suggestion on how to proceed with ferreting out qualified professionals begins with a warning on avoiding asking for recommendations from the municipal land use staff. Even if their policy does not prohibit their making recommendations, it does not mean such a recommendation has any relationship to professional ability, it more likely is due to just personally liking a consultant.

With regards to finding attorneys contact the local bar association for attorneys specializing in land development, do not expect them to express an opinion about an attorney, it would be viewed as unethical of them. Also, if there is a local directory of attorneys, it should include the services typically offered.

When you are interviewing surveyors and engineers and have not yet selected an attorney, ask what attorneys specializing in land use they hold in regard. Also, if you are in contact with realtors ask what attorneys developers use for subdivision projects.

To find potential land surveyors and civil engineers active in subdivision work in those municipalities where you are looking for property, you need to research the land records of the Town Clerk for each municipality. Specifically, you need to review the map index for residential subdivisions filed over the past several years to gather the following information.

**Subdivision Map Index Search:**

A.) Name of the consultant practice

B.) Type of practice:

1. Land surveying practice

2. Engineering practice
3. Practices offering both surveying and engineering

C.) The total area and number of lots in the subdivision
D.) Subdivision name and location
E.) Date the subdivision was approved and date of filing in land records

With the above information you can compile a chart as to the number of subdivisions and their size which a practice has performed. On the assumption that the most active practice(s) are the most successful in obtaining approvals you have your list of potential practices to consider.

When considering a practice providing both surveying and engineering, please keep in mind that some practices offering both may not be as accomplished in land surveying as a practice solely providing land surveying. This is the result when a practice initially established as an engineering practice, later adding surveying as a support to the engineering services, has principal(s) although also licensed as land surveyors, often do not have the same level of expertise as a practice offering only land surveying.

Upon being ready to choose your technical consultants and if they are separate practices, not a combined surveying and engineering practice, I recommend designating one of them as the project manager for all technical services, you do not want two qualified professionals each trying to be the leader of the project.

When close to your final choices discuss with each your choice of the project leader and ask if the other is comfortable with the arrangement. Advise your attorney of your choice.

If you are planning to create an ongoing development business beyond your initial subdivision, you need to become actively involved in developing your understanding of all aspects of development so you can effectively manage your future projects for success and highest profitability. My expertise herein will provide all the tools you need for you to do so.

## CONSULTANT INSURANCE

### OVERVIEW

It is important that your consultants have Errors and Omission insurance to protect you. It will provide you with protection from errors, omissions, mistakes, or blunders, that unfortunately can be made even by professionals.

It will cover the scope of the various services involved in your subdivision, whether investigatory, design plans, surveys and maps, construction estimates of material quantities and their cost for preparation of bid documents, and any other services they perform on your behalf.

## QUESTION TIME

Ask the professionals you are considering if they provide client protection with a "Professional Errors and Omissions Insurance Policy" (a.k.a. E&O)? If not, ask if they are willing to obtain such coverage if selected. If they are willing, keep in mind the possibility that they may quote their services at higher rates to compensate for the expense. If not willing to implement the insurance coverage focus your consideration on other consultants who do.

**During your evaluation of engineering and surveying consultants, you should inquire as to:**

A.) What are the coverage limits of their E&O policy
B.) Amount of policy coverage, per claim, all claims
C.) Deductible
D.) How many years with present insurer (if a brief time, prior providers)
E.) The status of any current claims
F.) Any claims in the past ten years? The outcome
G.) Ask for a copy of their E&O policy for your attorney and insurer to review

## FINALLY

Have a written agreement with your consultants that they and their insurer shall provide written notice to you if their policy premium is overdue, or the policy is being terminated by either party. I recommend that you have a discussion with your attorney as to the following:

A.) Whether you could have any exposure upon completion of all contracted services if a third party made a claim post services
B.) If a consultant or the insurer terminates their E&O insurance coverage while providing services to you, whether you could have any financial exposure for a third party filing a claim
C.) Ascertain whether the policy insures you after completion of services if the policy is terminated by either party.

# CHAPTER 5

## PROJECT MANAGEMENT

### OVERVIEW

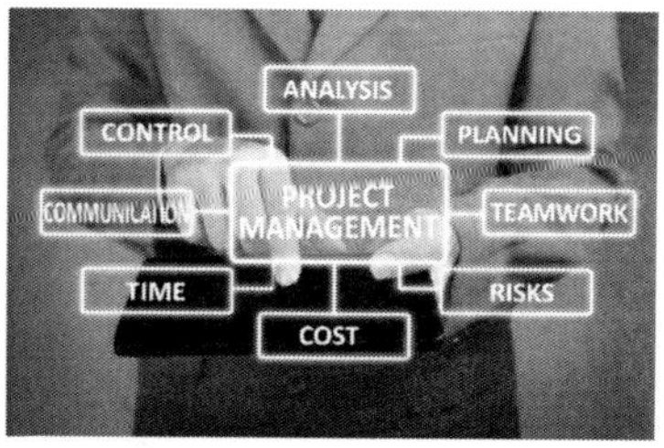


Project management is key to a successful subdivision, period. Basically, if you meet or exceed the deadline dates set at the beginning of the project with your professional consultants and stay within your budget, you will very likely be a winner.

Staying on schedule to meet deadlines is best managed by creating a project Timeline, which can be established by your consultant land surveyor and civil engineer upon their hire and continuing through the entire project until the subdivision's completed infrastructure is accepted by the municipality.

A budget is the other companion to the timeline, in effect a financial schedule of estimated expenditures, when the expenditures are to be made, then additional prearranged borrowing is required, and accurate, frequent financial tracking reports.

The budget will not be able to be set until both subdivision plans have been completed and your consultant engineer has prepared a line-item estimate of infrastructure improvement expenses. The selected contractor bid would then likely require minor adjustments to the budget.

### TIMELINE

So, what is a Timeline? A Timeline is a linear schedule of all services to create a subdivision. For each service: there is a start date; dates to complete certain of its stages; and a completion date. The timeline can be a digital software application or handwritten hard copy, both accomplish the same goal, time management.

A key point for you to understand about a timeline is that it consists of multiple timelines, each service has its timeline, and here is the key point I want to make, there will be constant overlap of work on the various services, it is comparable to complex multitasking.

The timeline scheduling can only be set by your professional consultants as it is they, who define the needed work, understand the sequencing of work, and the time to complete each of the various services, resulting in the efficient creation of your subdivision.

The only deadline date that you may have the ability to have your consultants agree to, is the submission date of the subdivision application to the Planning and Zoning Commission.

It is your responsibility as the project owner to also monitor consultant progress in meeting the various project deadlines, so obtain your own timeline schedule from them. If it is a digital software application find out if it can be live time updated.

Additionally, you should have a separate timeline for the administrative functions you need to be working on, such as: selecting a site contractor; your realtors marketing plan; finding a homebuilder or two to buy a discounted lot; finding a homebuilder to fronting a lot; utility installation policies, cost, etc.; and other functions to be addressed.

The same timeline process should be used with your site contractor for the installation of infrastructure improvements. It should be finalized with the contractor and your engineer weeks prior to the anticipated date of subdivision approval, allowing for quick startup of construction.

Missing your Timeline deadlines may result in unfavorable events affecting your subdivision, such as:

A.) Losing part or all of a seasonal or regulatory construction period
B.) Subdivision competitors beating you to market
C.) Finance rate increase
D.) Additional lending availability
E.) The lot and/or housing absorption rate decreasing
F.) Construction materials shortages, and/or increases in their cost; etc.

## RISK

Risk is directly associated with meeting or exceeding timeline deadlines and staying in compliance with your project budget. Adhering to timeline deadlines diminishes or eliminates the possibility of, or severity of, certain risks. Several prudent risk controls are:

A.) Adopting a conservative projection of lot sales gross income
B.) Adopting an infrastructure construction budget with a buffer, for unanticipated work and/or increases in materials costs.
C.) Borrowing money in stages versus entire amount upfront, reducing loan interest
D.) Jump start cash flow by selling one or more lots to an established quality home builder at a discount.

E.) Hold off final paving of the road wearing course and its expense until most of the home building is finished, heavy construction vehicles and off-road equipment can necessitate numerous, significant patching repairs to the binder course, better it than the wearing (top) course.

## BUDGET

The bulk of your budget for a subdivision with one or more internal roads will be for installation of infrastructure improvements. The earlier expenses of due diligence and contract deposit will be relatively minor in comparison, while investigations and design of the subdivision will be the second largest component of expenses.

If your subdivision has no proposed roads then the site improvements are likely minimal, a completely different and smaller budget.

Wherever your subdivision falls between these two extremes, the budget must be established, monitored, and adhered to for maximum financial success.

The budget should both be monitored in line-item format and as an overlay on a duplicate timeline chart, visually matching scheduled infrastructure installations with scheduled payments for installation services which have been inspected and approved.

# CHAPTER 6

## BUYER DUE DILIGENCE: POST SIGNED CONTRACT PART ONE – ALWAYS INVESTIGATE

### OVERVIEW

Once you have received the Purchase/Sale Agreement signed by the Seller, it starts the due diligence clock for investigations necessary to determine if the property can reasonably be expected to meet your requirements a viable subdivision.

As the due diligence period for performing investigations is typically a window of 10-30 days, you need to have prearranged with your consultants a schedule to accomplish them in a timely manner. This is the primary due diligence versus the basic one that was performed prior to submitting an offer to purchase.

What follows are the most common areas needing investigation, it is possible that one or more may not apply to your property, or that there could be specific investigations not mentioned that need to be performed as advised by your consultants.

## MARKETABLE TITLE

Marketable Title provides reasonable assurance to the Buyer that there are no encumbrances or a threat of litigation affecting a property ("a cloud") such as, but not limited to:

### TITLE SEARCH CRITERIA

A.) Chain of title, determines if there are any irregularities in the title
B.) Differing deed descriptions as to property boundaries and/or area
C.) Interests of others, including an option to purchase
D.) Adverse possession claim
E.) Notice of a violation of zoning law

F.) Liens and any notices of a Lis pendens
G.) Mortgages in default

Marketable title is provided to the Buyer by the Seller in Connecticut at Seller expense, other states may have a different policy. Typically, it is provided a day or two before the property closing, unlike closings for homes where it might be provided at the closing.

If it is unable to be provided by the closing, the Buyer contractually has the option of agreeing to a an extension of the closing date if it is reasonable to expect favorable Seller resolution in a short period of time, or of voiding the contract and receiving all deposit monies back.

In voiding a contract for purchase of a building lot, the return of deposit monies makes the Buyer pretty much whole other than for your attorney fees and time spent on finding the property. For a failed home purchase even with deposit monies returned, the Buyer will have greater financial losses due to having a home inspection, water testing, sanitary system inspection, etc., and may also have their existing home either under contract or already sold.

However, the losses associated with a failed house closing pale in comparison to the financial losses a Buyer faces when unable to close on a property which has gone through the subdivision process with the substantial expenses and time involved in obtaining approval.

This potential financial disaster can virtually be eliminated by addressing marketable title as the first step upon Buyer receipt of a Seller signed Purchase/Sale Agreement before being locked into moving ahead with the technical work and expenses necessary to subdivide the property.

The marketable title investigations by being moved to the front of the process versus the end, shall be performed by the Buyer, with the Buyer paying said expenses, and the Seller agreeing to make reimbursement to said Buyer at the closing.

Just before the closing a very brief inspection of the land records will be made to verify and update the marketable title of the property. This can be made by either the attorney of the Buyer or Seller with reimbursement of the Buyer if the party performing the update.

If either marketable title inspection discloses a problem that cannot be satisfied, the Buyer shall promptly receive both the return of all deposit monies and reimbursement for investigation expenses paid by the buyer. Upon receipt of the reimbursement and deposit monies the Buyer shall provide the Seller with documentation of the marketable title flaw(s). If the Seller fails to compensate the Buyer's investigation expenses or return the deposit, Buyer should immediately move to have a lien placed upon the property.

## ZONING

Zoning is one of the most important regulatory tools of a municipality, the others being the subdivision and inland wetlands regulations. All have their areas of control upon the land of a municipality. Zoning's purpose and focus is defining the uses permitted upon each type of property and the density of development of specified areas of the municipality.

The entire land area of a municipality is divided into areas known as zoning districts. There may be only one or two districts in rural municipalities versus many in non-rural municipalities. The boundaries of all zoning districts are depicted on the Official Zoning Map of the municipality and described in the zoning regulations.

Each district lists its permitted uses of the land and what are referred to in Connecticut as, "bulk standards", which are criteria such as, location of structures on a lot, minimum area of lots, height of structures, structure setbacks from property lines, and numerous other standards which apply to both existing property and future developments.

The zoning regulations of various municipalities will have many similarities but also unique aspects, so for each municipality where you are looking for land to develop, review their regulations, don't assume uniformity.

**The Types of Land Use Can Be Few or Many – Some Common Types of Use:**

A.) Residential – single family, multifamily, condominium, apartments, seasonal, trailer park, etc.
B.) Commercial – retail, restaurant, service station, mall, office, etc.
C.) Water Dependent – marinas, yacht clubs, boat repair facilities, boat storage, etc.
D.) Industrial – manufacturing, recycling, warehouse, quarries, asphalt plants, etc.
E.) Agricultural – farms, orchards, livestock, equine facilities, etc.
F.) Public facilities – parks, town hall, libraries, schools, community centers, cemeteries, etc.
G.) Religious facilities – churches, temples, schools, cemeteries, etc.
H.) Parks, open space, and recreational areas, etc.
I.) Forestry – logging, sawmills, waste wood by-products, etc.

**The Zoning Regulations Establish Specific Standards of Every Zone, Such As, But Not Limited To:**

A.) Minimum parcel widths and depths
B.) Areas excluded from meeting minimum parcel area such as wetlands and steep slopes

C.) Structure setbacks from property lines
D.) A specific geometric shape that must fit within the parcel
E.) Number of structures permitted on a parcel
F.) Minimum and maximum square footage of the entire structure and the structure footprint
G.) Maximum number of structure stories
H.) Maximum structure height

**Zone Designations:**

Each zone has a unique symbol, such as, R for residential, C for commercial, A for agricultural, etc. Zones can have sub zones, such as, R-20, R-40, C-20, C-100, A-5, A-20, etc. For the R and C zones the numeral is the minimum area in thousands of square feet, and for the A zones the minimum area in acres.

**The Boundaries of Each Type of Land Use Area Are Typically Described By:**

A.) Manmade improvements such as: roads, railways, canals, etc.
B.) Natural features such as: rivers, shorelines, etc.
C.) A specific distance from one of the features mentioned above
D.) Along a known property line or series of property lines

**Municipalities Without Zoning**

Are you at risk in developing a residential subdivision in a municipality without zoning? It depends. In Connecticut only three out of 169 municipalities lack zoning regulations and one of them is considering them. These three towns are amongst the most rural in a state with few true rural areas remaining. However, in your state, areas not rural may also possibly lack zoning regulations. Be sure to evaluate.

**Some Factors to Consider When No Zoning:**

A.) Will your prospective subdivision property when developed be profitable with sale prices comparable to the value of existing homes in proximity? If your homes were significantly higher in price, buyers may be concerned about their future value if lower price homes are built due to no zoning standards
B.) Can commercial or industrial uses be built adjoining it, or in proximity
C.) Can public service facilities, such as, transfer stations or sewage disposal plants be constructed in proximity

# ENVIRONMENTAL HAZARDS INSPECTION

## OVERVIEW

One of the most important investigations during the **Due Diligence** period is to determine If any environmental hazards exist on the property. This Is especially important for developments where on-site individual or community wells will be the potable water source.

A recognized professional in environmental matters should be hired to perform an inspection and prepare a written report of the findings. The initial and hopefully only level of inspection to be required, is a Phase One investigation consisting of both a review of public environmental records of the area, plus a site inspection.

## INSPECTION

**Phase One**. Your environmental consultant reviews the public data base of the state, county, regional, and municipal information, and then commences a site walk of your property.

If the review of the public data base indicates a concern with an adjoining property, if owner permission is granted to walk the property a better understanding of what risk it may or may not be to your property.

If no environmental risks are discovered, then the investigatory phase is concluded, a wrltten report shall be provided to you, and you should be confident that this concern is eliminated.

However, if an environmental concern arises in **Phase One**, then further investigation of the property is necessary, this is known as **Phase Two**. This phase will entail investigating the subsurface soils to determine: the boundaries of the contamination; the type of contaminant(s) and the degree of contamination. A written report and any supplemental documents will be provided to you. The report may include a recommendation on methods to remediate the contamination and a best estimate of the time and cost.

**Remediation.** If you are still interested in the property, make purchase subject to remediation satisfactory to you, and that the property owner is the responsible party to remediate the environmental problem, this eliminates your involvement and risk.

Your contract should include the ability for you to terminate it, either upon completion of Phase One or Phase Two if unsatisfied with the results, and to promptly receive the return of your deposit money.

### INQUIRY

A prudent additional step is to have your consultant inquire of municipal regulatory staff if any properties, even at a significant distance to your subject property have, or have had, an environmental hazard, such as: service stations with leaking fuel storage tanks; chemical plant leakage, and other industrial contaminants and ascertain if a potential risk exists to your property. If your consultant feels a risk may exist or is uncertain, you have the choice of additional investigation or terminating the contract.

### ACTUAL CONTAMINATION ISSUE

As a case in point, I had a client in Connecticut with a prospective property for subdivision, to be served by on-site individual wells. It was disclosed during preliminary project meetings with Town staff, that a service station in the area had for many years an underground fuel tank leak before its discovery. The station was about a mile distant from the property of interest to my client.

Contamination had reached properties close to my client's property of interest, but on the opposite side of the State highway on which his property fronted. Initially upon hearing this, my client was going to terminate the purchase/sale contract, however there was an extensive State monitoring well system in place for several years, from the service station to the general area of my client's prospective subdivision. Monitoring had determined the contamination boundaries, and monitoring data indicated that clean-up had both reduced the degree of contamination and that it was not progressing closer to my client's property of interest.

My clients for additional comfort hired a groundwater consultant to work with State agency technical staff to determine what risk, if any, existed to future ground water wells on my client's prospective property, resulting in a determination that the State decontamination program eliminated the possibility of contamination migrating into the groundwater of the prospective property, so my clients proceeded with a successful subdivision approval and development.

## EASEMENTS – RECORDED AND PRESCRIPTIVE

### OVERVIEW

Easements are of two types, either a written document (deed) describing the rights a party has with respect to another party's property, and recorded in the land records for public notice, or a prescriptive easement.

Prescriptive easements are almost universally unknown to exist by a property owner, they are discovered when a land surveyor is performing a property survey.

## RECORDED EASEMENTS – WRITTEN

Easements can be viewed as positive, neutral, or negative depending upon the purpose of the easement; its location upon a property; whether perpetual or for a specified period of time; and the perspective of the party burdened with the easement.

If the existence of a deeded easement is discovered during the "Preliminary Due Diligence Prior To Contract Submittal," the deed description may be insufficient to determine its location without the expertise of a land surveyor.

It is the function of the land surveyor when performing a property survey to determine the location of an easement through one or more of the following:

A.) A deed description

B.) Existing maps of the property or adjacent properties, both recorded and unrecorded

C.) Physical evidence of the easement located during the field survey

D.) Testimony of present and past property owners and parties acquainted with the easement

When the location of an easement is determined it shall be depicted on a property survey map with appropriate geometry to permanently define its location.

For a property you are considering purchasing, if it has a recorded easement which grants a right or use to an adjoining property, a determination should be made as to whether it has an undesirable impact on the proposed subdivision. If it does, investigate whether it is feasible to obtain its abandonment, or the relocation of the easement or a portion of it, subject to the approval of the easement beneficiary.

## PRESCRIPTIVE EASEMENTS – UNWRITTEN

This type of easement becomes established upon a property by use of a portion of the property by one or more individuals without the permission of the owner, meeting the minimum time specified for such establishment by the General Statutes or case law of the respective state.

The reason most prescriptive easements become established is either because the property owner does not inspect or monitor the property and is unaware of its use by others or is aware of its use but takes no legally required action to terminate said use.

For a property where the owner is unaware of its use by others, the use is most often discovered during a site inspection of the property by a potential buyer's consultant land surveyor. When a property survey is performed, the property map besides indicating the location and area of a possible prescriptive easement, the apparent use also needs to be identified, such as, pedestrian, equestrian, vehicular, or other use(s).

The next issue then is to determine whether the easement meets the statuary period for establishment. It requires attempting to determine when the use began.

**Some methods to determine when use began:**

A.) Testimony of property owners adjacent to, or in proximity to the subject property
B.) Testimony of a prior owner(s) of the subject property
C.) Aerial photography taken over prior years or decades
D.) Claims of the user(s) of the prescriptive easement
E.) Determination by a court

If the use has no impact on the development of a subdivision you may choose to ignore it. If its location affects a proposed subdivision layout or creates a potential liability issue and is discovered either before submitting an offer to purchase or during due diligence, consultation with your attorney is advised. If its discovery comes during the subdivision design process or after closing on the property, and its continued use is a problem, your options are to either obtain agreement on its termination or a partial or complete relocation, if feasible.

Prescriptive easements are often of narrow width, such as: a footpath; an equestrian trail; or the piping of water from a spring, while an old farm vehicular road can be fairly wide. However, some prescriptive easements can be quite large, such as an area used for agricultural or livestock purposes, this happens more often on extremely large, vacant properties in isolated areas of a municipality.

A potential prescriptive easement may exist in plain view, as when a municipal highway department clears trees and brush on private property along a road without permission, to create and maintain improved vehicular sight line (comparable to a view easement) for a road.

**Is there risk of a prescriptive easement becoming a claim for adverse possession?**

Adverse possession claims need to meet the following three criteria: open and notorious use; continuous use for the State statutory period, and no attempt by the owner to terminate said use. So, if a prescriptive easement exceeds the statutory period for a claim of adverse possession, the possibility exists that a suit for adverse possession could be instituted by the user(s) of the prescriptive easement. Discuss this matter with a land use attorney.

## F.E.M.A. FLOOD ZONE

### OVERVIEW

The **Federal Emergency Management Act (F.E.M.A.)** has established flood hazard areas throughout the United States. They are depicted and identified on a series of maps known as, **"Flood Insurance Rate Maps (FIRM),"** as various **"Special Flood Hazard Areas (SFHA)."**

The SFHA defines the various levels of flooding risk for a geographic area by zones which are depicted on the FIRM with a description of the potential flooding risk of each zone. Insurance rates for a property located in one of the flood hazard zones are based upon the degree of flooding risk for that zone. Flood insurance is not mandatory but is advisable for a homeowner to reduce the risk of severe financial exposure. Flood insurance is for structures, not land, and should be anticipated as a mandatory requirement of lenders for a property in a flood zone.

### SITE SPECIFIC

When evaluating a prospective property for a subdivision it is especially important to determine whether any portion(s) of the property is in one or more of the various flood zones, as proposed home construction will need to conform to appropriate mandated design criteria for the zone.

New home construction must meet or exceed the **Base Flood Elevation (BFE)** for the zone in which it is proposed to be constructed. The BFE is defined as the lowest floor elevation of the structure, and that definition includes basements. In shoreline developments this can result in the need to construct homes raised on pilings to meet thc BFE.

Keep in mind that the more severe the flood zone area(s) is, the zones construction criteria to meet the BFE may mean that potential house siting locations on a lot may be quite limited and could entail higher construction costs. Consult with your land surveyor and/or engineer to better understand the BFE impact on a property before submitting a purchase offer.

A concern developers should be cognizant about is that the ongoing climate changes can be outpacing the mapped boundaries for flooding, especially in low lying coastal areas and inland areas protected by levees which potentially are subject to being breached, especially those designed based upon criteria from decades ago.

## ABANDONED AND DISCONTINUED ROADS

### OVERVIEW

Why be concerned about that narrow, rutted "travelled way," frequently called a "farm road" or a "woods road," on a property being considered to purchase for a subdivision. It may appear to be not much more than a disused farm road internal to the property, or an road from colonial days bounded with fieldstone walls on each side, it may have numerous trees in its travelled way making it unpassable other than by foot, or relatively open but with no apparent sign of vehicular use.

To answer the status of a road believed to be, or have been a public road, then a determination must be made as to its existing legal status. In Connecticut road status is generally resolvable by investigating the land records of the Town Clerk of the municipality for information in the Town Meeting volumes for actions taken or not taken on a road.

### INVESTIGATION

**Classification Index of Municipality's Roads:**

A.) Improved and maintained roads
B.) Unimproved roads
C.) Abandoned roads
D.) Discontinued roads

Alternatively, information on roads may often be found in the Engineering Office, the Public Works Department, or with the Road Superintendent of the municipality.

**Roads With Unknown Name – Possible Resolution Sources:**

A.) The records of the local historical society or town historian
B.) Superseded tax maps of the Assessor from decades earlier
C.) Earliest versions of the U.S.G.S. topographic maps ot the vicinity
D.) Town and county atlases of the 19th century
E.) Ancient maps located in the State Library

## Procedure to Abandon or Discontinue a Road

Abandonment or discontinuance of a municipal road must likely as in Connecticut, be similar in other states, requiring a public meeting as specified in the Charter or Ordinances of the municipality. Upon approval at said public meeting, a description of the action taken would be published to notify the public and recorded in the Town Clerk's office in a volume specifically dedicated to Town Meetings or a similar purpose volume.

Locating a record of a specific abandoned or discontinued road would likely commence with a search of the Index of Town Roads or Former Roads. If such an Index does not exist, then the only option is to search the Town Meeting volumes for the time period believed to include action on the road, or if no approximate date is known, then all Town Meeting volumes will need to be researched.

## ABANDONED ROAD

For a road to become abandoned, the governmental entity whose road it is, whether municipal or state, surrenders its rights to the road forever, which terminates its use by the public.

The road right-of-way is divided along the travelled way centerline with the property owners on each side of the centerline receiving that portion of the abandoned right-of-way which adjoins their property. All owners for which this road provides access from/to a public road continue to have a right to pass and repass upon the abandoned road travelled way to their property.

If a proposed subdivision development has frontage on an abandoned road and it is the only potential access from a public road, the ability to upgrade it to meet the current public road standards to serve your subdivision, will require both the agreement of all property owners between its junction with the existing public road and the point where the upgraded road would be entirely on the subject property.

Additionally, these other property owners would also need to agree to convey sufficient land for the construction of a road meeting the current road right-of-way width standards for roads per the subdivision regulations and/or road ordinance standards. This road would be subject to approval by municipal regulatory agencies and acceptance of it post construction by the municipality.

## DISCONTINUED ROAD

Whereas for a discontinued road the respective governmental entity has closed the road to the public but has not relinquished its ownership, there is no transfer of land to the adjoining landowners. The road may in the future be reopened to the public or abandoned, all property owners for which it provides access from/to a public road retain the right to pass and repass to their property.

A discontinued road being upgraded to the current municipal road standards for a subdivision may only require approval by the municipal regulatory agencies with jurisdiction if all construction improvements and minimum road right-of-way width can be met within the existing boundaries of the discontinued road.

If sufficient width to meet current standards does not exist, then as mentioned above in an abandoned road situation, one or more adjoining property owners would need to be cooperative in conveying the necessary land.

## REGULATORY AGENCY STAFF CONSULTATION

### OVERVIEW

Prior to both submitting a purchase offer on a property or commencing subdivision design of the subdivision, it is important to meet with the regulatory agencies staff to determine if there are any matters besides the published agency regulations that might affect your subdivision.

If you have decided to meet regulatory agency staff prior to submitting your offer to purchase, be circumspect about identifying the specific property you are interested in, instead ask questions that are applicable to the general area where the property is located.

Why this caution? The caution is because if you identify the specific property prior to having a Seller signed purchase/sale agreement, innocent office staff comment about it amongst their colleagues may be overheard by a visitor to the office, such as, a developer, attorney, builder, realtor, etc., and that information may result in someone going to the property owner and obtaining a signed purchase agreement leaving you with a lost opportunity.

This is a possibility whether the property is unlisted or listed with a realtor. Several clients of my Connecticut consultant practice over many years had it happen to them, including one of my earliest clients who switched to my firm after his consultant engineer with whom he discussed the property before having a signed contract, unethically went to the owner and obtained a contract for the property. There is no recovery from this very unfortunate event, after all you had no written agreement. A WWII merchant marine and navy phrase comes to mind, “loose lips sink ships,” very appropriate.

The above should not discourage you from having a discussion with regulatory staff which can be very informative before submitting an offer to purchase, just keep your discussion general, absolutely not specific to the property until you have a signed purchase/sale contract.

## NOW FOR STAFF INTERROGATION

Key Questions of Staff to Determine if You Should Make an Offer to Purchase

**With respect to the general area where the property is located:**

- A.) Proposed change of zone
- B.) Proposed change in permitted uses
- C.) Changes to Plan of Development
- D.) Any proposed non-residential development in area
- E.) Any ground water contamination, particularly if subdivision to be served by wells

With respect to the regulations, standards, and ordinances applicable to subdivisions, are there modifications to the following regulations, and are they: approved with an effective date; before a regulatory commission for action to consider; or in an informal discussion stage.

## REGULATIONS, STANDARDS, ORDINANCES OF:

- A.) Zoning
- B.) Subdivision
- C.) Inland Wetlands
- D.) Conservation or Environmental
- E.) Health regulations for subsurface sewage disposal systems
- F.) Road design standards/ordinances
- G.) Storm water management standards
- H.) Lastly, ask if any other regulation(s), etcetera, applicable to subdivision development

The staff responses to all the above will help you make an informed decision whether to proceed with an offer to purchase, modify your offer, or end further consideration of the property.

Once you have a signed contract for the property a return visit to regulatory agency staff by yourself and your consultants is mandatory to discuss specific aspects of your proposed subdivision and hear any concerns or questions of the staff. A conceptual layout sketch would be most helpful in discussions, “a picture is worth a thousand words.”

Follow up all meetings with a summary letter of the meeting prepared by yourself or your consultants, sent to the respective agency staff members. This is important as you should not assume they are keeping a written record of discussions at meetings. Anticipate written staff correspondence only after submission of a subdivision application.

## UTILITIES

Utilities such as water, gas, electricity, cable, and telephone are provided by, and installed by, private utility companies, or the municipality, or regional authorities, or the subdivision developer.

However, subdivision storm water road drainage and possibly public sewage systems, are generally not viewed as a utility. Both are likely installed prior to the afore mentioned utilities by the developer.

**The developer is responsible for contracting for the installation of utilities by each provider, and providing certain other associated services, such as:**

A.) Grant of any required utility easement(s)
B.) Easement map(s)
C.) Surveyor set easement boundary markers

**Utility providers for the subdivision will specify in their contract several key matters, such as:**

A.) Installer of each utility
B.) Method of installation and whether above or below ground
C.) Payment for utility equipment and its installation when required
D.) Construction bonding (if any)
E.) Ownership of each utilities installation
F.) Responsible party for maintenance and/or replacement of each utility.

Installation of utility services for individual lots is not part of the contract for installation of utilities in the subdivision. The subdivision developer if building the homes, or the lot owner if using another building contractor, would be the responsible party.

**NOTE:** Extension of Utilities to Subdivision. Some properties may not have some or any of the necessary utilities running along the existing road the property fronts upon, requiring their extension to the proposed subdivision road. As the utility extension(s) will be along an existing public road, depending upon the specific policy of each utility provider, the subdivision Developer may or may not be responsible for some or all the expense of the extension(s).

## SEWAGE DISPOSAL

### OVERVIEW

There are three methods for serving a subdivisions sewage disposal requirement, a public sewage system, individual lot on-site subsurface sewage disposal system, or a community system(s) serving some lots or the entire subdivision.

The factors that will determine which method is to be used are: if a specific system is required by the municipal subdivision regulations; there is no public sewage system in proximity to the property; or the sewage treatment facility lacks sufficient capacity for additional inflow, the last two situations necessitate on-site subsurface sewage disposal.

### Public Sewage System Served Subdivisions

From my consultant experience these systems were always installed by, and paid for, by the developer. It is possible that in other jurisdictions that a sewer authority may do the installing, all costs are likely either born by the developer or assessed against each lot, payable upon purchase by a buyer.

A subdivision with suitable terrain conditions (elevation variations) will allow for installation of a gravity system, while a subdivision having terrain with minimal elevation variations or a site lower in elevation than the sewer trunk line will need a pump station(s) to raise the sewage up to the elevation of the trunk line.

Municipal regulations and/or the State Health Code may require a subdivision to be served by a public sewage sewer system when available, even if suitable soils for individual lot subsurface sewage disposal systems exist in the subdivision. The individual lot hook-up to a public sewage system and its cost is the responsibility of the lot owner if the home is not being built by the developer.

Two issues during the buyer due diligence period specific to soils testing are: a.) that at this time there is no preliminary lot layout to know where to perform meaningful soil testing, and b.) the due diligence period is probably not long enough to do more than a few random tests. So, it is especially important to have in your contract a purchase price adjustment clause to guard against loss of lots due to unsuitable soil test results, in addition to other potential issues.

Both of the following types of on-site sewage disposal require soils testing to substantiate that there are both suitable soils and sufficient area for the subsurface system.

### Individual Lot On-Site Subsurface Sewage Disposal Systems

These systems are the only alternative for developing a subdivision when a public sewage sewer system is not available, or the sewage treatment facility is at capacity. An adequate area on a lot with soils suitable for this type of system must exist along with a reserve area of similar capacity for possible replacement in the future.

### Community Subsurface Sewage Disposal Systems

This type of system is typically used when contiguous lots in a portion of a subdivision lack suitable soils for individual subsurface sewage disposal systems on their respective lots, and where there is no public sewage sewer system available.

An area in the subdivision with suitable soils would need to be developed with a subsurface sewage disposal system designed to serve the requirements of all lots to be connected to the system. This system would be installed and paid for by the developer, however the gravity and/or pump feeder line(s) from these lots to the system, along with the system itself, would be the responsibility of the lots served to maintain, service, and eventually in the future replace if necessary.

An association separate from any overall subdivision association would be established specific to these lots served by the system, also the parcel of land containing the system would be deeded by the developer to this association.

## FIRE PROTECTION

### OVERVIEW

The developer is responsible for installing an adequate water supply system for fire protection of the homes of the subdivision.

The water supply system for subdivision fire protection is typically provided by one of these methods:

A.) Municipal, private provider or developer water system

B.) Fire ponds, either natural or created

C.) Fire water storage tanks.

All these various fire protection methods are to be installed and paid for by the developer. The method(s) to be used in a subdivision will either be specified in the subdivision regulations or determined on a case-by-case basis by the Planning and Zoning Commission or by the municipal fire authority.

**Municipal, Private Provider, Developer Water System.**

Fire hydrants are connected to the water supply system of the subdivision, the spacing between fire hydrants is determined by the municipal fire authority.

**Fire Ponds.**

They may be naturally occurring or excavated by the developer, both may be recharged either by ground water or by connection to an adjacent waterbody. Drought conditions may require supplementing the water supply by water tanker truck.

**Fire Water Storage Tanks.**

Storage tanks became popular in Connecticut subdivisions as there generally is no public water supply in suburban areas, and few natural fire ponds, nor always suitable soils with water recharging capability.

Storage tanks were specified by regulations to be underground installations, but I assume there is no reason that they couldn't be above ground installations elsewhere, excepting areas of the U.S. with severe winters. Two benefits of storage tanks versus fire ponds are that there is no evaporation factor and no water loss due to porous soil. The tanks are filled as needed either by the fire department, public works department, or a contracted water supply firm such as a pool water company. A draught pipe is installed in the tank to facilitate ease of access by the fire department to hook-up to a pumper truck.

## WATER RIGHTS

### OVERVIEW

Water rights can be held by a third party having legal access to your water, or your property may have rights to access the water of other properties. Rights can be for either subsurface water or to a waterbody. These rights can be private agreements between parties, typically described in a property deed or other legal document, or as agreed to in a compact between several states, most typically in Western states.

A potable water supply is mandatory for residential subdivision uses and is also necessary for many commercial, industrial and agricultural uses, with recycled water being used more and more in many non-residential situations.

Vast areas of the United States, particularly in the West and Southwest are semi-arid and/or nearing maximum use of available water from waterbodies, rivers and aquifers. This has resulted for proposed property development, including residential subdivisions, either demonstrating that the property has a sufficient potable water supply for all proposed lots, or limiting the number of lots based upon the permitted water usage for the property as established by a regulatory agency.

Separate from the water needs for the purposes of the above various entities, is the recreational use of, and the aesthetics of, waterbodies contained within or adjoining a property, and the increased real estate value due to access or views. So that wonderful view and planned use of a waterbody should not be taken for granted in evaluating a prospective property, it requires land records research to substantiate whether a third party has rights which can negatively impact the view, use, and the perceived increase in property value. See, "Now Back to Water Rights", on the next page.

## IS MORE STRINGENT WATER ACCESS REGULATION ON THE HORIZON?

I won't go into what are, or probably will be more stringent water access rights in the Western U.S., but the general newscasts on the topic paint a difficult situation of insufficient water supply for all users. Therefore, anyone planning subdivision development in this part of the country needs to consult with professionals as to what the present and long-term water access situation will be, for any property you are considering.

During my professional consultant career and personal life in Connecticut I've only experienced two types of water issues. One was a condition of approval for my subdivision by a Planning and Zoning Commission that a well with adequate yield and water quality had to be drilled prior to obtaining a building permit for constructing a home. Typically, builders leave both the well and subsurface sewage disposal systems to the final stage of building, however, based upon well records of surrounding subdivisions, it indicated that wells on my subdivision might require well depths of 400 to 800 feet to meet the minimum yield requirement.

## NOW BACK TO WATER RIGHTS

This water issue was not connected to my consultant practice or development business but to personal real estate property, one was a land tract I owned, the other was a small lake with seasonal cottages, both affected by water rights in favor of others. One property was for my personal residence, I saw the property during the wetter part of the year and put it under contract, as a consultant land surveyor I saw tons of property, some nice, some not special at all, this was a very special picturesque property. The West River, not as significant as it sounds ran north to south through the middle of the property, some 34 acres, it was a 20-foot width watercourse except in the summer months when it shrank to a10-12 foot width with a maximum depth of 2 feet. It turned out when I was performing surveying services several years later on a property upstream to mine, that the U.S.C.&G.S. map indicated a reservoir on a water course which fed into the West River upstream of my property, this reservoir discharged no water in the summer months, a contributing factor to my and neighboring properties low water. Digging into the land records I found that the water company had many decades ago acquired the rights to the water flowing into the reservoir and the rights of downstream properties to said water flow.

A second property with a water issue was a summer cottage on a small lake I considered buying. It was located on a dammed pond with many other cottages. I saw the cottage in the winter but decided to hold off until summer. When I returned in summer the water level had dropped significantly, exposing about 50 feet of pond bottom beyond the winter shoreline. It was very unattractive in appearance and looked as though it could be difficult to get out to the water. Research of the land records determined that the water rights to the pond had been acquired decades ago by a manufacturing plant several towns downstream, it used the water to run their hydroelectric facility to power much of the plant. I passed on buying the property.

So, be careful and never assume that water bodies are free of rights in favor of others.

## SUBDIVISION STATE HIGHWAY ACCESS

### OVERVIEW

If your prospective subdivision is on a state highway, any proposed subdivision road needing access and egress from said highway, will require not only approval by the municipal regulatory agency, but most importantly approval by the State highway department.

**CAUTION.** If municipal regulations don't require that you obtain some degree of State approval before municipal approval, I strongly suggest you ignore the ability to seek municipal approval until you have obtained the **"best assurance of future State approval"**, because if the State doesn't agree with the location of the municipal approved subdivision road junction with the State highway, you won't get State approval, thereby making the municipal approval meaningless.

During my years as a consultant designing subdivisions, many of them required access/egress from a Connecticut State highway, I found the following to be good advice, **"don't put the cart before the horse,"** the State is always in the driver's seat, not the municipality.

My reference to the afore mentioned phrase, "best assurance of future state approval," is because the Connecticut State Highway Department does not approve and issue a permit to connect a proposed subdivision road to the State highway until the municipality grants final approval of the subdivision.

The **"best assurance"** as to what you will be able to obtain and provide to the municipality typically is a letter from the State that the plans have preliminary approval, with final approval dependent upon receipt of a revised plan incorporating requested plan modifications, and a copy of the municipal subdivision approval.

## AREAS OF STATE INEREST AND CONCERN

As part of obtaining preliminary State approval, the State will field inspect the area of the proposed subdivision road/highway junction with your engineer or surveyor to discuss the four principle matters which are always their main concern.

### Adequate Sightline Stopping Distance:

The minimum sight line distance for highway traffic to safely stop to avoid entering traffic from the subdivision road (applies to both directions and is a function of the posted speed limit) and for traffic on the subdivision road to safely enter onto the State highway.

### Subdivision Road Storm Water Drainage:

The State will either require:

A.) Retention – No discharge from the subdivision onto the State right-of-way or drainage system

B.) Detention – Discharge permitted onto the State right-of-way or drainage system after the post storm water peak has passed

### By-Pass Lane and Deceleration Lane(s):

**By-Pass Lane.** To be installed to the right of the highway thru lane, permitting thru traffic flow to continue by using it when vehicles on the thru lane are stopped or slowing prior to making a left turn into a subdivision road on the opposite side of the highway.

**Deceleration Lane.** To be installed to the right of the highway thru lane, permitting thru traffic flow continuing on the thru lane when vehicles are slowing to turn right into a subdivision road on the same side of the highway.

**Traffic Signal:** State traffic studies will indicate if there is a need for a traffic light at the junction of the subdivision road with the State highway; if a traffic light is to be required, the developer should anticipate paying for it.

Your permit to make the required improvements in the State right-of-way will be issued upon receipt of municipal approvals of the subdivision, including plans and reports pertinent to the subdivision road/highway junction, the posting of a performance bond of a type and amount specified by the State, and appropriate contractor liability insurance.

An as-built plan of the installed improvements may be a condition of the State to issue a letter certifying that all work is completed per the plans and is satisfactory, allowing the release of the State performance bond. The State letter will also be necessary before the municipality will accept the subdivision road as a public road and release any balance of the performance bond for the subdivision to the developer.

# IMPACT FEES

## OVERVIEW

Unlike Connecticut where I had my consultant practice designing subdivisions and developing them personally or in partnership, other states or political jurisdictions may have a requirement for payment of fees by a developer to address the impact of a subdivision on the community due to the necessity of additional public services to be provided, including construction of new facilities.

## PUBLIC SERVICES

As there are a multitude of probable public services, such as, police, fire, emergency services, schools, libraries, community centers, parks, athletic fields, roads, sidewalks, etc., impact fees might be a significant dollar amount, especially if most, or all have to be paid upfront upon subdivision approval or commencement of its construction.

**Impact policy should describe construction subject to impact fees, and how fees are determined;**

A.) Percentage of the purchase price of the subdivision land
B.) Percentage of the cost of the subdivision infrastructure improvements
C.) Percentage of the combination of the above two methods
D.) Percentage of the appraisal valuation of the completed subdivision
E.) Flat fee for every subdivision lot or house
F.) Percentage of the actual cost of providing services and/or construction of facilities
G.) Any other method established by a regulatory agency

Understand the potential of impact fees before making your offer to purchase or include a contract clause to adjust the purchase price up or down from a base impact fee estimate to account for the final impact fee determination.

## PROPERTY ASSESSMENT INCREASE

### OVERVIEW

Developers of Connecticut subdivisions understood that an increase in the value of a property as a result of subdividing it would also result in an increase in the assessed valuation of the land, and therefore an increased tax bill.

Connecticut taxation of real property is by each municipality based upon the assessment valuation of said real property by the municipality's Assessor.

Generally, regarding land, there could be one or more assessment valuation increases as a vacant land tract eventually becomes through the subdivision process approved building lots.

### ASSESSMENT INCREASE SEQUENCE

The first assessment increase was generally very minimal and was tied either to the recordation of the deed of purchase or of the approved subdivision map in the municipal land records. The next increase, or it might be the first increase, was potentially the largest jump in the assessment valuation of the land.

Depending upon the municipalities policy, it would either be upon significant completion of the road infrastructure of the subdivision and the ability to sell lots and obtain building permits for home construction, or acceptance of the subdivision roads as town roads, when this valuation increase would take place.

In a large subdivision the road system was generally not constructed in its entirety, or bonded in its entirety, but built in phases so as to control construction costs until income from the sale of lots and/or completed homes in earlier phases was available to defray subsequent road construction expenses.

The above process required several months for the first phase of development and many months or years before the final phase(s) were completed. Phased development resulted in manageable assessment increases and tax bills for the Developer, which were anticipated in the financial projections for the project.

So, if where you are considering developing a subdivision, the assessment policy of the municipality is similar to the above, all very likely is well and good.

**CAUTION.** The importance of understanding a municipality's assessment policy for subdivision lots cannot be stressed enough. Here's what happened to my largest developer client, it was not due to negligence on his part.

My consultant practice had recently obtained approval of my client's subdivision of several hundred acres, a huge project for southern Connecticut. Its development would require several years as road locations were in difficult terrain requiring substantial blasting of ledge. This was a project with a long timeline of several years for completion

Just before the approval of my client's subdivision a new Assessor for the Town of Killingworth, Connecticut came into office and immediately upon approval of the subdivision sent a block buster of a letter. He stated that upon approval by the Planning and Zoning Commission the entire subdivision was subject to an assessment increase from raw land to its value when all infrastructure was installed.

The Assessor claimed the ability to increase the assessment based upon approval of the subdivision before my client even closed on it and before its recordation in the land records.

With years of infrastructure construction expenses ahead, it would be a couple of years before any positive cash flow from lot sales would arrive for my client.

My client sued both the Assessor and the Town of Killingworth, it was closely watched by other developers, most holding off on initiating subdivision applications unless they were quite small or had no roads. Unfortunately, his lawsuit and appeal were not successful, the Assessor's interpretation of assessment rights per State statutes was upheld.

This outcome of significant increased property taxes much earlier in the project would be potentially destabilizing for many developers, fortunately my client was also a major site contractor which helped to reduce actual cash outlay for infrastructure improvements, which helped moderate the impact of tax situation. My client further moderated the tax situation by beginning building homes for additional revenue, eventually the project was a highly successful subdivision financially.

So, do not fail to understand the property assessment policy of all municipalities you seek to develop in.

# CHAPTER 6

## BUYER DUE DILIGENCE: POST SIGNED CONTRACT PART TWO – INVESTIGATIONS IF APPLICABLE

## ENCROACHMENTS

### OVERVIEW

Property line encroachments can be either by an adjoining property or your prospective property. In nearly all instances during my career as a consultant land surveyor in Connecticut, I found clear physical evidence by observation as to which property owner was responsible for encroaching upon their neighbor's property. A few times I was not able to determine by observation which property owner was the encroacher, in that situation questioning the respective owners might lead to resolving which one was the encroacher. However, if not resolved between the owners, the only solution is legal action.

### INTENTIONAL AND UNINTENTIONAL ENCROACHMENTS

**Intentional Encroachments**. They are the most blatant, what defines them are a wide scope of activities, such as: debris piles; old autos, trucks, boats, and farm equipment; construction materials; cutting trees for firewood; firewood splitting operation and stockpiles of unsplit and split firewood; livestock activities; Christmas tree raising; sheds; and hazardous materials, amongst other activities.

**Unintentional Encroachments**. Generally, they are the result of one or both adjoining property owners either not knowing where a property line is, or believing they do, but being wrong. Most unintentional encroachments are due to a lack of knowledge as to where the property line is located, most commonly the situation between adjoining lots in a subdivision.

If you have a prospective property in your sights, you need to guard against an encroachment being discovered after you receive back the seller signed purchase contract. Why you say, because the seller may take the position that by not including encroachment resolution as a condition in your offer to purchase the property, that you are buying it “as is”, and that it will be your responsibility to resolve.

To preclude this situation your offer to purchase should include a condition that the Seller is responsible for addressing encroachments discovered at any time prior to the property closing, to your satisfaction. The Sellers attorney shall also send written notification to the encroacher to end the encroachment and to remove whatever has created the encroachment.

If the Seller is encroaching on a neighboring property, the same approach as described above should be a condition of your offer.

### CAUTION – LAND GRABBING

A most serious type of encroachment can only be described as “land grabbing,” the intentional removal of property line monumentation by an adjoining property owner and resetting the monumentation into the interior of the neighboring property. In my 30 plus years surveying in Connecticut I only found this type of encroachment twice. This type of encroachment would most likely only be discoverable by a land surveyor during a property survey.

The owner of the property encroached upon should immediately forward the property survey map to their attorney and have a notice to desist sent to the encroacher. The property survey map should immediately be recorded in the municipal land records and the surveyor should be instructed to set monumentation at the correct locations. Consider billing the encroacher for the additional work.

## BOUNDARY LINE AGREEMENTS

### OVERVIEW

The purpose of a boundary line agreement is to resolve the location of a common boundary between property owners that is either unknown to them or its location is disputed by one or both. Resolution as to the location of this common boundary will either be by mutual agreement by the property owners or by a court determining its location.

Whichever way a boundary line agreement is reached, it requires that deeds describing the change(s) be executed and recorded in the land records of the municipality.

## TECHNICALITIES FOR RESOLUTION

Boundary line agreements often have land both conveyed to the other property and land being received from the other property. The respective areas conveyed out and received are not necessarily equal areas. It is also possible that one property is the sole conveyor out of property, and one the sole property receiver.

Two methods are available to create the required deed description of the location of the new common property line based upon the boundary line agreement.

**Parcel Exchange Method.** It is dependent upon having made a survey of the entire apparent common property line including both land that is in dispute and any land not in dispute. One or more new boundary lines are proposed by the surveyor and/or an attorney.

If the owners reach agreement on a new boundary line, a boundary line agreement map is prepared by the surveyor depicting those parcels of land to be conveyed by or between owners with parcel geometry to prepare deeds to effect the transfer of land and the creation of the new boundary line. The boundary line agreement map and all descriptions of the parcels to be deeded are concurrently recorded in the land records.

Future deeding of the entirety of either property to third parties will not involve description of these individual parcels but instead the new common property line.

**Release of Claim Method**. This method effects a new boundary line using the same map as in the parcel exchange method, proposed boundary options, and agreement on one boundary by the owners. That is where the commonality ends.

There are two options with respect to creating the new common boundary line. One is quite simple, a release of any claim by each owner upon any land on the opposite side of the new boundary line and recording both releases concurrently in the land records. The other option is dependent upon current property survey maps being available of each owner's property incorporating the new common property line and creating new deed descriptions of each property based upon the boundary line agreement and recording the deeds and maps concurrently in the land records.

State statutes may specify a different requirement for a valid boundary line agreement exchange, check with your attorney or land surveyor. I strongly recommend that if a boundary line map is not required that one be prepared and recorded concurrently with the deed(s) for clarity, a picture is worth a thousand words.

**Cautionary Comment.** During my years as a Connecticut consultant land surveyor, I had a unique situation involving my client's property and a "boundary line agreement" between my client's predecessor and an adjoining property owner.

Upon research of the land records to begin a property survey of my client's property, I located a filed "boundary line agreement map." The intent of this map was to depict an area of the adjoining property to be incorporated into the property of the late husband of my client. No deeds of the land exchange depicted on the map had been recorded, however the map was signed by both property owners, and both were now deceased. The area depicted on the "boundary line agreement map" subsequent to being filed, resulted in the runway of my client's privately owned airport being extended upon it.

The other property to the "boundary line agreement" had subsequently been sold by the other map signatory. However, the deed of conveyance was based upon a prior deed by which that signatory had acquired the property. This deed only had a partial, metes and bounds description of its property lines, nor made mention of that portion of the property "conveyed out" per the "boundary agreement map," to my client's late husband.

From observation It appeared that the present owner of the property likely considered the limit of useable land which ended at a marsh area which separated the rear portion of their property from the extended runway as the general area of the common property line and assumed that that the runway was entirely on my client's property.

This "boundary agreement area" had been occupied by the extension of my client's runway for many years, with my client potentially having, or soon having the ability to file legal action for a claim of adverse possession. Also, potentially in the interim a prescriptive easement might presently be in effect.

I advised my client of my findings and suggested that they immediately consult with their attorney before proceeding with any designing plans for the airport.

The key point to remember is that only a deed can convey real property, not a map.

## WHAT'S BURIED? WHAT CAN BE BURIED?

### WHAT'S BURIED?

Hopefully, your property of interest is found to be pristine, however properties can have past burials which may not be easily discernable to the inexperienced, requiring professional investigation to determine location and what is buried.

If a site walk of the property discloses suspicious areas such as: a heavily wooded property with a cleared area with no topsoil and/or soils not normally at the surface; a mound not appearing to be a natural terrain feature; debris, in particular construction materials; seepage at the surface or on a slope and it's not water; empty or full drums or containers; or other questionable items, definitely have an environmental consultant check out the property.

Your environmental consultant as part of making a Phase One investigation of the property, typically a thorough site walk of the entire property preferably after having a meeting with the appropriate municipal staff regarding any environmental history or concerns they have about the property. The State Department of Environmental Protection (DEP) also is appropriate to be contacted.

A Phase One investigation should always be done for your peace of mind that you are not buying a pig-in-the-poke property with the financial responsibility to clean up any environmental problem(s). Also, if you anticipate requiring some financing for the property purchase, development expenses or bonding, all lenders want to see a clean Phase One report.

**Some Concerns of Municipalities and Lenders Are:**

A.) Hazardous materials affecting the environment
B.) Buried materials requiring removal due to conflict with proposed infrastructure/home construction
C.) Contamination of ground water, especially serious when wells are necessary for development
D.) Existing burial locations of permitted materials not in compliance with zoning or other regulations

## WHAT CAN BE BURIED?

The zoning or subdivision regulations or municipal ordinances will be specific as to what type of debris from construction of the subdivision infrastructure or construction of individual homes can be buried on-site, and where it can be located.

**Common Prohibitions in Connecticut Municipalities:**

A.) Burning of tree debris and brush
B.) Burial of tree trunks not suitable as timber or firewood,
C.) Burial of stumps and brush

The latter two are a serious concern due to leaching into the ground water, especially when homes will be served by wells. Also, the possible subsidence of the earth due to their decomposition.

Stumps are generally prohibited from burial; the best solution is to have a stump grinder brought on-site and either bury its ground remains or dispose of it off-site.

**So, What and Where is Burial Permitted?**
Generally, rock, boulders, unsuitable soils (excluding topsoil), masonry waste from on-site construction, and other non-hazardous materials not subject to decomposition (settlement issues) or contamination of ground water are pretty much what is permitted to be buried.

The most common burial location is the area on individual lots between the property lines and the zoning building setback lines. It may also be permitted in an open space area if it has an existing open field where no structures are permitted or proposed to be constructed.

## COASTAL ZONE MANAGEMENT PROGRAM

### OVERVIEW

The purpose of this program Is to "identify coastal resources and minimize or even deny activities which degrade a costal resource.

Within the National Ocean Service (NOS), as part of the National Oceanic and Atmospheric Administration (NOAA) is the Office for Coastal Management (OCM) which manages the voluntary federal-state partnership to, "protect, restore and responsibly develop within the nation's coastal communities and resources".

All 23 coastal states excepting Alaska, the 8 Great Lakes states, and the 5 U.S. territories participate in the National Coastal Zone Management Program. Excluding the 5 U.S. territories, 31 states which meet the program criteria are participating. At the end of this topic is a complete listing of the states.

Each State has implemented regulations which are approved by NOAA and has designated a specific State department or agency to administer its program. As there are likely different approaches to accomplishing its goals, I'll speak specifically about Connecticut where some of my consultant practice clients' projects were within the program area.

The Connecticut legislature approved the "Connecticut Coastal Management Act of 1980", which was also approved by NOAA in 1980. The program is administered by the Office of Long Island Sound Program within the Department of Energy and Environmental Protection.

**Connecticut has a two-tier system defining its coastal zone**

**The first tier, the "coastal boundary"**, is defined per Sec. 22a-94 (b) of the Connecticut General Statutes and is further defined as, "the contour elevation of the 100 year frequency coastal flood zone, as defined and determined by the National Flood Insurance Act, or a 1,000 foot linear setback measured from the mean high water mark in coastal waters, or a 1,000 foot linear setback measured from the inland boundary of tidal wetlands mapped per Sec. 22a-20, whichever is farthest inland".

**The second tier, the "coastal area"**, is defined per Sec. 22a-94(a) of the Connecticut General Statutes and "includes all the land and water within the state's 36 coastal municipalities" (of 169 total), of which 24 municipalities have direct frontage on the shoreline of Long Island Sound (LIS), and 12 municipalities which lie inland of LIS being affected by tidal waterbodies.

Connecticut requires for proposed development within coastal zones, a "Coastal Site Plan Review Application", of which two of its components are: "Coastal Resources Identification" and; "Coastal Use Policies Identification", the specifics follow.

**Coastal Resources:**

- General Resources (applies to all sites and uses)
- Beaches and Dunes
- Bluffs and Escarpments
- Coastal Flood Hazard Area
- Coastal Hazard Area
- Coastal Waters/Estuarine Embayment's
- Developed Shorefront
- Freshwater Wetlands/Watercourses
- Intertidal Flats
- Islands
- Rocky Shorefronts
- Shellfish Concentration Area
- Shorelands
- Tidal Wetlands

**Coastal Use Policies:**

- General Development (applies to all sites and uses)
- Boating
- Coastal Recreation and Access
- Coastal Structures and Filling
- Cultural Resources
- Dams, Dikes and Reservoirs
- Dredging and Navigation
- Energy Facilities
- Fisheries
- Fuel, Chemical and Hazardous Materials
- Open Space and Agricultural Lands
- Ports and Harbors
- Sewer and Water Lines
- Solid Waste
- Transportation
- Water-Dependent Uses

If you have a proposed subdivision project which is within the coastal boundary zone of any of the states listed below, consult with either your land surveyor or engineer to assure your plans will be in compliance with all pertinent criteria and regulations.

## Coastal (Ocean) States:

Alabama California Connecticut Delaware Florida Georgia Hawaii
Louisiana Maine Maryland Massachusetts Mississippi New Hampshire
New Jersey New York North Carolina Oregon Pennsylvania Rhode Island
South Carolina Texas Virginia Washington

**Great Lakes States:**

Illinois Indiana Michigan Minnesota New York Ohio Pennsylvania Wisconsin

**Note:** The states of New York and Pennsylvania are unique in that portions of both states are located within both the Coastal (Ocean) and Great Lakes zones.

## NATURAL RESOURCE RIGHTS OF OTHERS

Developing subdivisions focus on the surface of a property, however in many parts of the country, rights to the subsurface natural resources of a property may reside either with the property owner or a third party.

For any resources intended to be retained by the owner, you may want to attempt to negotiate the termination of those rights as a condition of your purchasing the property.

If resources are controlled by a third party you have a situation where if you believe the resource extraction impact unfavorable with respect to the enjoyment of the property by your future lot/home buyers, you either are going to have to be if prepared to pay for release of those rights or to not proceed with considering the property.

Subsurface resources rights include minerals, oil, gas, and water both surface and subsurface. Several things need to be determined if a prospective property is subject to any such rights and whether perpetual or time limited, and if limited whether to a specific quantity or volume.

For a property without a public water supply system, determine if the owner, a third party, have rights to the water. If either or both do, you need to determine whether you will acquire a guaranteed volume of water with the purchase of the property sufficient for the anticipated number of lots in your subdivision. If there is no proposed guarantee it is obvious that you need to end consideration of the property.

If oil or gas are the subject right, and drilling is ongoing, until drilling is finished and less invasive extraction installation(s) remain, subdivision development may not be feasible from a marketing perspective if the property is significantly impacted, turning off potential buyers.

Mineral extraction rights have two methods of operation, strip mining from the surface down to the mineral sought and tunneling. The former in my opinion is always a walk-away, the overburden is always left on the property, not a pretty sight. The later may not be a walk-away if there is minimal blasting which is not sensed on the surface, no processing of the mineral or storage of waste on-site.

Just be careful in considering a property with natural resources rights to be retained by the seller or held by a third party they have the potential to be a project killer.

## ABANDONED OR DISCONTINUED RAILROAD AND TROLLEY LINES

You may be evaluating a property and find that it has either a railroad or trolley line right-of-way running through the property. When the rails have been removed it most likely indicates that the rail line has been abandoned versus discontinued.

The difference between abandoned and discontinued is use. Abandoned means the permanent end of use of the rail line while discontinued means the ability exists for its use to resume.

However, the trolley lines I am speaking of were the intrastate and interstate trolley systems of decades past; if a right-of-way was discontinued, for practical purposes they are effectively though not legally "abandoned," as unlike a discontinued railroad line, trolley systems have virtually no viable prospect to resume operations.

Abandoned does not mean that "ownership" of the right-of-way has been terminated, only that the right to operate rail service has been permanently terminated by the operator. The current "ownership" of the rail line right-of-way is dependent upon how it was initially acquired.

If the property burdened with the right-of-way has no legal right to cross the right-of-way, the property is effectively two properties, with each section of the property needing independent access to a public road for the possibility of any development.

However, depending upon how the right-of-way was acquired, irrespective as to whether for a railroad or trolley line, access to the portion of the property on the far side of the right-of-way may be possible as follows:

**Abandoned Rail / Trolley Line:**

A.) Ability to cross the right-of-way is dependent upon the Grantor having reserved said right

B.) If no rights exist to cross, fee purchase of a portion of, or all the right-of-way may be an option

**Discontinued Rail / Trolley Line:**

A.) As the line is potentially subject to being reopened to rail traffic, fee acquisition of a crossing may be unlikely, instead a grant of an easement is likely the only potential option the owner might consider.

B.) A road crossing of the right-of-way by an easement, may eliminate it from becoming a public road in certain municipalities.

**Note**: If an at-grade crossing of the right-of-way is not permitted, the alternatives of bridging or an underpass will require significant engineering and construction costs.

If abandonment of a rail line is determined upon research of the land records of a municipality, the method of the right-of-way acquisition is key to determining both the present owner of the right-of-way, and whether adjoining property owners have the right to cross over the right-of-way.

## RIGHT-OF-WAY STATUS UPON ABANDONMENT

| Initially Acquired As | Present Owner/Right Holder | Adjoining Owner(s) Rights |
|---|---|---|
| Fee Simple (Purchase) | Railroad or Trolley Co., or its successor | No Fee Interest; Rights only if reserved at conveyance |
| Easement | Railroad or Trolley Co., or its successor; or the Grantor | Fee if successor to original owner if easement terminated; if not, only rights if reserved |
| Licensee (Right of Use) | Railroad or Trolley Co., or its successor; or Licensor | Fee if successor to original Licensor; if not, only rights if reserved |
| Eminent Domain (Condemnation) | Railroad or Trolley Co., or its successor; or original owner or successor | Fee if successor to original owner and state statutes require reversion; if not, only rights if granted at condemnation |

**CAUTION #1** The status of an abandoned rail or trolley line and the rights or lack of rights of the burdened property and/or adjoining property should be determined by consultation with your attorney. The layperson should not attempt to interpret State statutes and/or case law affecting abandonment.

**CAUTION #2** Determination of the location of the boundaries of a rail line right-of-way is often difficult for the land surveyor to resolve, as the initial mapping and monumentation may have been insufficient and/or monumentation may over the decades been destroyed or disturbed. The resultant may only be the ability to designate a boundary as approximate, which may require resolution by a boundary line agreement or a court.

## CROSSING ACTIVE RAILROAD LINES

A property which can only be accessed for development by crossing an active railroad line should be evaluated extremely carefully before submitting a purchase/sale offer. The process to determine whether to do so, requires a significant amount of time and is usually very expensive.

**Methods of crossing a rail line:**

A.) At-grade
B.) Bridging
C.) Underpass

**These two factors will determine which method will be used:**

A.) The railroad company's policy on crossings
B.) Terrain and soil conditions at a proposed crossing

For all methods, the railroad will only grant an easement to cross its right-of-way, the access road on each side of the right-of-way easement will be either publicly or privately constructed and owned on non-railroad property.

At-grade crossings are the highest risk crossings for accidents, best suitable for rural or low traffic volume locations. They are the simplest to install, the developer is responsible for the costs of the improvements which can be all, or some of, the following: road/pedestrian safety gates; warning lights; railroad signalization; roadway/track grading match, and street traffic light(s).

In Connecticut and possibly for the entire AMTRAK system, their policy is to not permit new at-grade crossings, and to eliminate all such crossings where alternative access is feasible. This was to facilitate the introduction of the Acela high speed rail service from Boston to Washington, D.C., with overhead electrification. The only options to create a new crossing of the AMTRAK right-of-way in Connecticut, is either by bridging it, or by an underpass.

Underpass crossings require a track bed which is either significantly higher in elevation than the surrounding terrain for an at grade road to be constructed underneath, or if the track bed is of moderate elevation above surrounding terrain, a road which can be depressed below the surrounding terrain to cross under the track bed, but only if storm water can be drained from the low point of the road. Underpasses require stabilization of the track bed for safe passage of trains during construction.

Bridging a rail line, whether the track is in a cut, at grade, or at a higher grade than the surrounding terrain is similar to a road overpass being constructed over a lower road. Whether a proposed crossing is by bridging over a track in a cut, or a track having a similar or higher elevation than surrounding terrain, abutments for the bridge span would need to be constructed outside of the railroad right-of-way. Placement of fill and possibly retaining walls for the fill, are typically necessary for the road to match the elevation of the bridge abutments.

## CLIENT PROJECT TO CROSS AMTRAK – A SERIOUS CAUTION

During my professional career as a Connecticut land surveyor I had a client project requiring the crossing of the main AMTRAK line between New York and Boston, in Guilford, Connecticut. Only by doing so, could access be provided to a parcel of land with views of Guilford Harbor and more distant views of Long Island Sound. Access to this property would provide the ability to build a substantial number of expensive homes. Access was to be obtained by a proposed bridge crossing the AMTRAK right-of-way. A crossing involved constructing a short section of road requiring fill and a retaining wall between an existing public road to the proposed bridge abutment. A similar situation was required on the opposite side of the railroad right-of-way from the bridge abutment back down to existing grade to proposed internal roads serving the subdivision. This road was to be a permanent cul-de-sac road as the property was surrounded by a protected saltmarsh. The Town of Guilford stated that it would not accept a road extension as a public road, as it would be a further lengthening of the existing permanent cul-de-sac public road, from which the access road was to commence. Additionally, the town wanted no future responsibility for maintaining or replacing a bridge over a two track, high speed, overhead electrified rail line.

The only option was that the entire road extension and bridge system would need to be privately owned and maintained by a homeowner's association of the proposed subdivision established by the developer. In addition to the annual maintenance costs the association would need to fund, the Town wanted to guard against the association not adequately setting aside funds for the eventual repair or replacement of the bridge and coming to the Town for financial help.

The Town therefore required my clients to seek approval of a Special Tax District for their proposed subdivision to specifically levy and collect funds to maintain and replace the bridge and the private roads of the subdivision. The above would have to be successfully resolved prior to consideration of an application for subdivision; additionally, my clients were to provide initial funding of the homeowner's association.

To seek a crossing approval from AMTRAK the process required my clients to provide plans of the bridge design and modification of the overhead electrification system under the bridge, both to 60%-70% of final design, before AMTRAK would consider issuing a letter committing to granting an easement, subject to later approving final plans. Multiple visits to AMTRAK'S Philadelphia offices were necessary as designs proceeded, due to several AMTRAK personnel changes during this process, new design requirements were made by the new AMTRAK personnel, necessitating additional meetings and review.

So, at this point my clients had expended a substantial amount of money and time, obtaining only a verbal commitment for a grant of an easement, and were also having a problem with the property owner who was seeking either a closing before final approval by AMTRAK, or an additional substantial non-refundable deposit, so my clients opted to terminate the project. A lot of money and time down the drain.

## WATERSHED AND SUPPLY WELL PROTECTION

### POTABLE WATER SUPPLY PROTECTION

Potential contamination of a potable water supply is a concern when a proposed subdivision development has no public sewage sewer system access, instead being served by individual subsurface sewage disposal systems.

Protection of potable water sources is the responsibility of an Aquifer Protection Agency which requires the mapping of the recharge areas of both existing and prospective well sites and regulates proposed activities in these areas.

Residential subdivisions proposed in proximity to recharge areas and to be served by individual subsurface sewage disposal systems must demonstrate that their effluent will not contaminate the recharge area.

### WELLS

Water providers protect their wells from contamination by establishing a protection zone around the well. The protection zones size is related: to the volume of water the well is designed to withdraw; the porosity of the soil for groundwater recharge, and its travel time to the well. An analysis must be made for each subsurface sewage disposal system in proximity to the well protection zone that bacteria in its effluent will be eliminated before reaching the well protection zone. Compliance is determined by an analysis which determines the necessary minimum distance for the sewage effluent to be bacteria free, and that this distance is less than the distance to the well protection zone.

## WATERSHEDS

There is a major difference in the protection areas for watersheds versus wells, the former can be hundreds, thousands, and in some instances tens of thousands of acres while the later in comparison is a relatively modest area immediately surrounding the well.

Watersheds typically include watercourses, and surface water which drains from uplands immediately adjacent to a reservoir, minor tributaries to it, and any major watercourse flowing into a dammed reservoir. The watershed boundaries for feeding the reservoir are typically the ridge lines of the terrain surrounding the reservoir, beginning at the dam, and continuing upstream of the reservoir.

Water providers, whether a private company or a public authority have produced maps of well protection zones and protection limits for reservoirs and their watersheds. They will be found at the water providers offices and in the land records of the municipalities where the providers facilities are located.

# TRAFFIC STUDY

Throughout my practice area consulting for developers of subdivisions, no municipality's subdivision regulations included a requirement for a traffic study.

However, if a Planning and Zoning Commission during the subdivision application presentation believed there was a traffic concern, they had the ability to request a traffic study. The commission would defer action on the application until the report was received.

Only a few of the substantial number of subdivisions I designed over a career of 30 years were required by the Planning and Zoning Commission during the application presentation process to have a traffic study performed, most the result of neighbors alleged problems.

**Factors Which May Require a Traffic Study:**

A.) Extremely large subdivision
B.) Located in a densely developed area
C.) Significant commercial traffic on the area's road network
D.) If there is existing heavy commuter traffic
E.) If the existing roads do not meet the current road standards to safely manage an increase in traffic
F.) Complaints that increased traffic will negatively impact quality of life and property values.

If a traffic study is requested, a traffic engineer is the recognized professional to perform it. The study will also determine the day(s) and time(s) with the highest traffic volumes, typically Friday afternoons are generally the highest volume of traffic. Recommendations will be made in the report as to viable solutions to alleviate or moderate the impact of increased traffic generated by the proposed subdivision.

**Possible Solutions for Anticipated Traffic Increase:**

A.) Traffic signalization
B.) Additional traffic signage
C.) Street lighting
D.) Intersection improvements
E.) Resurfacing roads
F.) Widening sections of road
G.) Deceleration and/or by-pass lanes
H.) Some local streets converted to one-way

# CHAPTER 7

## PROPERTY INVESTIGATIONS

### BOUNDARY SURVEY AND MAP

A boundary survey is generally the first major technical service performed to begin work on your proposed subdivision.

Your surveyor begins with research of the land records followed by a field survey to locate physical evidence of the boundaries of the property. This information along with the deeds and maps from research of the land records are the base information and documents for office analysis to determine the boundaries of the property and create a boundary survey map.

The boundary survey map later becomes the base map for most other individual maps and plans, such as, a inland wetland boundary map, a topography map, and a "Existing Conditions Plan".

The next two services generally performed are the location of the boundaries of wetlands, if present, and preparation of a wetland boundary map, and a topographic survey to create a topographic map of the property for any required engineering design.

The boundary survey map, wetlands boundary map, and topography map will be compiled to create what is commonly known as, the "Existing Conditions Plan." This plan becomes the basis for the design of the lot layout, roads, and other required plans. You should now become involved with your surveying and engineering consultants in reviewing their suggested subdivision layouts and discuss the pro and cons of each layout. However, if this is your first subdivision and you are beginning with a small land tract, there may be only one obvious layout.

For subdivisions to be served by individual on-site sewage disposal systems a fourth key investigation is necessary to finalize lot and road locations, this is soils investigation on all lots to determine suitable areas for these systems.

**Key steps in creating a subdivision.**

**Research of the Land Records (Excluding Financial) To Determine:**

A.) The ownership of the property
B.) Any cite in the property deed of an existing property survey map
C.) Boundary line agreements
D.) Easements
E.) Leases
F.) Lis pendens
G.) Any other recorded burden upon the property

**Physical Inspection of the Property Boundaries For:**

A.) Location of evidence of the boundaries of the property
B.) Encroachments upon common boundaries by an adjoining owner
C.) Possible prescriptive easements
D.) Internal roads/travelled ways crossing from adjoining property

**Maps and Plans:**

A.) Boundary (Property) Survey Map
B.) Division Map (if applicable)
C.) Topographic Map
D.) Wetlands Boundary Map (if applicable)
E.) Existing Conditions Plan
F.) Subdivision Map
G.) Site Development Plan
H.) Road and other infrastructure plans
I.) Other maps or plans required by a regulatory agency or your consultants

## WETLANDS BOUNDARY DETERMINATION

### OVERVIEW

For those states such as Connecticut which have both inland and tidal wetlands, both are regulated for activities proposed within their boundaries and for a specific distance upland of said boundaries.

There are two separate but interrelated sets of statutes, regulations and applications for inland and tidal wetlands.

The regulations cover two principal areas, wetlands boundary determination and proposed construction activities within the regulated area. Regulations will specify if an activity is a "use as of right," therefore regulation exempt.

The regulatory agencies can be one or more of the following: the municipality where the property is located; the Department of Environmental Protection, generally only tidal wetlands, and the U.S. Army Corps of Engineers for any proposed activities in tidal waters and submerged land under their jurisdiction.

## Wetlands Determination – Boundary (Inland and Tidal)

### Inspection:

Properties must be inspected to determine if either inland or tidal wetlands exist upon the property by the recognized professional(s) of your state. For Connecticut, a soil scientist but also a botanist for tidal wetlands. Depending upon the state it may be determined by a different professional.

If wetlands are found from inspection, the wetlands boundaries are marked in the field for location by a land surveyor. The type(s) of wetlands soils are also determined during the field inspection and included in a report describing all aspects of the soil scientist's or recognized professional's investigation.

Depending upon the availability of staff and current policy of the Soil Conservation Service of the U.S. Department of Agriculture for the district where your property is located, they may be available to either field delineate the wetlands boundary of the property and provide a soils report of their investigation, or only verification of the boundary delineated by your soil scientist.

### Mapping:

A land surveyor will field locate the delineated wetlands boundary marked by the soil scientist or other qualified professional. If regulations also require field topography of the wetlands, it would likely for efficiency and cost control be performed while locating the wetlands boundary unless existing topography is available. If high precision aerial photography of the entire property has or will be performed, it would be the ideal source for topography.

### Application - Inland Wetlands:

For a mapped inland wetlands boundary to be recognized as the official wetland boundary of a property, an application to approve it as the official boundary must be submitted to the Inland Wetlands Commission or other designated agency.

The application process in Connecticut involves at the initial commission meeting acceptance of the application and a brief overview of the land surveyor's wetland boundary map before setting of a date for a site inspection by the commission members. The land surveyor and/or soil scientist would always accompany the members of the commission on the site inspection to answer any questions.

At the next meeting, the commission asks its members who inspected the property if they had any comments or questions regarding the site inspection. The land surveyor or soil scientist would be the party to respond to them.

The commission can then move to approve the application, making the soil scientist delineated boundary the official wetlands boundary of the property, superseding the existing boundary as depicted on the Official Inland Wetlands Boundary Map of the municipality.

**Tidal Wetlands:**

The Connecticut Department of Environmental Protection (DEP) has mapped the tidal wetlands boundaries of the entire state. However, as their boundaries are based upon interpretation of photogrammetry from high altitude aerial photos, not field investigation, for accurate determination of a property's tidal wetland boundaries, field delineation must be performed by a qualified professional such as, a soil scientist, botanist, or other recognized professional. It is advisable to have a representative of DEP confirm the boundary delineated by your professional.

**Note:** DEP has no application, just field confirmation by their staff of the boundary by your professional. However, the municipal Inland Wetlands Commission will want to review the delineated tidal wetland boundary while considering your inland wetland boundary application. They have no jurisdiction but are interested when tidal and inland wetlands are in proximity to each other.

Inform the commission of the type of professional that delineated the tidal wetlands boundary, and that DEP concurs with the boundary.

The tidal wetlands boundary would be depicted on its own map if no inland wetlands is in proximity. However, when both wetlands are in proximity to each other, they should be depicted together on a map or plan such as, the "Inland Wetlands Boundary Map" or the "Existing Conditions Plan."

**Regulated Activity - Inland Wetlands**

If the development of a property has any portion of the subdivision infrastructure improvements either within the wetlands proper, or within a specific distance upland of the wetlands boundary, detailed construction plans of each proposed activity are required as part of the application(s) for consideration of approval by the Inland Wetlands Commission.

**Note:** If any construction is proposed within the jurisdictional area of DEP for tidal wetlands, it would be depicted on its own construction detail plan, unless the activity is in proximity to inland wetlands, whence the proposed construction would be depicted on the same plan.

A regulated activity application cannot be submitted prior to approval of an inland wetland boundary delineation application. They can be submitted concurrently, however the boundary application must be approved prior to approving a regulated activity plan application. Generally, the boundary application is submitted earlier, as it can be ready before a regulated activity plan is designed.

As with the boundary application the Inland Wetlands Commission members will field inspect all proposed regulated activity site(s) to better understand what the impacts will be upon the wetlands, discuss whether there is an alternative to the activity, or a way to reduce the impact.

Prior to the inspection the land surveyor should, even if not required by regulations, layout the limits of each proposed activity area, this eliminates the possibility of only being able to identify the approximate location of an activity in the field from the plans which would prove embarrassing.

The land surveyor or engineer and the soil scientist for major proposed activities should accompany the commission members to guide them to each activity location, discuss each activity, and answer questions.

**CAUTION:** When developing adjoining properties, a number of years apart, that have a wetlands boundary that crosses the common property line of the properties, make sure to use the same soil scientist or environmentalist for delineating the boundary of both properties.

**Why?** On two adjoining properties I surveyed a few years apart, I was not able to schedule my regular soil scientist for the initial property, so instead I used another recognized soil scientist to delineate the boundary. A few years later my regular soil scientist delineated the boundary on the adjoining property. The resultant was that the boundaries of each property did not match in two locations along their common property line.

Upon noticing the boundary problem, I had both soil scientists meet in the field to reinspect the areas of disagreement. They came to an agreement upon reexamination of the soils in both disputed areas as to the proper locations. As the municipal wetlands staff does not compare adjoining properties delineated boundaries, likely because I was the same surveyor for both properties was the discrepancies found.

**Recommendation.** I strongly encourage using the same wetlands consultant to delineate the boundaries of adjoining properties, especially if not being delineated and surveyed at the same time

## TOPOGRAPHIC MAP

### OVERVIEW

Topographic maps depict the contours of a property, key information necessary for design of subdivision infrastructure improvements.

Individual lot development can also make use of the topographic mapping if of high accuracy for home siting and subsurface sewage disposal systems when public sewer systems are not available.

There are several methods of obtaining topography for a property, however a regulatory agency's standards may specify a specific method, if not, the choices should be discussed in consultation with your project engineer to select the appropriate method for your subdivision.

**Topography Types:**

**Aerial Photography – Low Altitude**

The most detailed topography as it is based upon photography flown at low altitude specifically for your subdivision by an aerial photogrammetry consultant

| | |
|---|---|
| Advantages | Very precise one-foot contours and spot elevations |
| Disadvantages | Photography flight windows can be limited in parts of the country to:<br>Late Fall/Early Winter – between foliage loss and first snow<br>Late Winter/Early Spring – after snow melt/before spring foliage |

**Aerial Photography – High Altitude**

Existing aerial photogrammetry flown at high altitude to encompass very large geographic areas, such as a county or even the entire state

| | |
|---|---|
| Advantages | No waiting for a seasonal flight window<br>Less expensive than a low altitude photographic flight flown of a specific property |

Disadvantages — Photography typically is taken several years apart so physical improvements are not always current.
Photography at a higher altitude results in lower precision contours and spot elevations
Not satisfactory for the one-foot interval contours needed for engineering design.

**NOTE:** Both of the above aerial photogrammetry methods may require supplemental field surveying for:

Confirmation of contour accuracy (prudent check)
Additional spot elevations
Missing contours and spot elevations in areas of dense conifer tree coverage

**Field Topographic Survey**

Physical on-site elevation survey

Advantages — Proposed infrastructure construction can have greater detail in critical areas

Disadvantages — Field survey is time consuming and labor intensive, more expensive, less precision generally the larger the property area
Coverage less thorough unless property mainly open and gentle terrain
Office survey processing of field survey data, time consuming and labor intensive unless surveyor has topographic processing software

**Compilation of U.S.G.S. Quadrangle Maps:**

Advantages — Readily available; individual map cost is very inexpensive

Disadvantage — The ten-foot contour interval is unsuitable for site design, useful only for preliminary planning.
Maps are from aerial photogrammetry that can be decades old.

**NOTE:** Contours from U.S.G.S topographic maps may be allowed for small subdivisions with no proposed infrastructure

# SOILS TESTING FOR SEWAGE SYSTEMS

## OVERVIEW

During the years, my consultant practice was designing residential subdivisions, the municipalities where I worked had no public sewage sewer systems, nor did they want them.

Both the town fathers and residents were consistently opposed to municipal sewage systems being advocated by the State of Connecticut as they fervently believed that if said systems were Installed, developers would attempt to modify the zoning regulations to decrease the minimum lot area and other standards, thereby increasing building density and traffic, and decreasing green space.

Therefore, all proposed subdivisions were served by individual lot subsurface sewage disposal systems, and very infrequently by a subdivision community sewage system serving a limited number of lots within the subdivision with unsuitable soils for individual sewage disposal systems.

Proposed subdivisions required soil testing to locate suitable areas on each proposed lot for a subsurface sewage disposal system and a 100% reserve area to guard against failure of the primary system decades in the future.

**Be Aware of the Following:**

A.) Does the public health code or subdivision regulations restrict soil testing to certain times of the year? Systems designed based upon testing during the dry season may fail in the wet season due to inundation by rising groundwater levels.

B.) Is a 100% reserve disposal area required? It guards against a possible future failure of the primary system.

C.) The minimum Public Health Code required separation distance between subsurface sewage disposal systems, a well, and house footing drains.

As soils can have variable characteristics from lot to lot, it may necessitate several types of sewage disposal system designs. This is addressed by determining the soil characteristics of a lot by excavating test pits in the proposed disposal area, and your engineer or soil scientist determining the soil characteristics profile for design.

**Typical Soils Profile:**

A.) Topsoil depth (stockpile to cover backfilled test pit)

B.) Fill material (not naturally occurring soil, if any)

C.) All soil types and depths of each layer

D.) Determining presence of any restrictive soil layers or water intrusion, such as:
  1.) Ledge or decomposed ledge
  2.) Clay and silt soils
  3.) Water infiltration seeps, depth of
  4.) Seasonal high ground water soil staining, depth of

With test pit soil profile data, plus a percolation test (soil absorption rate of water), and the number of bedrooms of a proposed home, the engineer has the required information to select and design the appropriate subsurface sewage disposal system for the lot

## ARCHEOLOGICAL AND PROTECTED FEATURES

### ARCHEOLOGICAL FEATURES

State law, or subdivision, conservation or historical regulations may require investigation of a property for archeological sites either by a data base search and/or field inspection.

Regulations will specify the type of professional qualified to investigate, in Connecticut this would generally be a degreed archeologist who will prepare a report documenting any findings, their significance, and whether permanent protection should be the goal.

The definition as to what constitutes an archeological site may not be uniform from one regulatory jurisdiction to another. It may include depending on what part of the country the property is in, prehistoric, first peoples of the Americas, native Americans, Spanish explorers prior to English colonization, French and Dutch trading posts, English colonies, and historical sites of all types. Even if your property is located where there are no such regulations, if such sites are found, consider that we are the caretakers of the land, the past is a great educator for all.

### PROTECTED FEATURES

Protected features are typically designated by municipal subdivision or conservation regulations and are intended to preserve certain natural features, or "historic" man-made features.

In a Connecticut town where I frequently designed subdivisions, fieldstone walls erected in colonial days were protected from random demolition. They could only be breached for installation of subdivision roads and driveway access into a lot, while placement of a home, pool, tennis court, sanitary system, well, and other improvements had to be designed to avoid or minimize wall disturbance.

Subdivision commissions have been known to influence applicants to agree to certain protections, such as for a magnificent ancient tree or a rare species tree, as part of conditions of approval even if not specifically covered in the regulations. So, you may want to be initiative-taking and bring such items to their attention, it may provide benefits to you in the approval process.

## EXISTING CONDITIONS PLAN

**The Existing Conditions Plan is a compilation of all the above investigations and their resultant maps, plans and reports.**

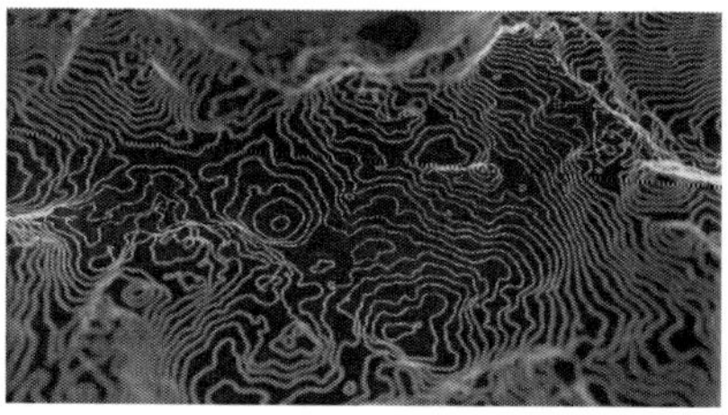

A.) Property Survey Map
B.) Wetlands Boundary Determination Map (inland & tidal)
C.) Topographic Map
D.) Soils Testing for Sewage Systems
E.) Archeological and Protected Features

This plan is most important as it is the entire base information for the final design of the subdivision. All these investigations may not be pertinent to every subdivision, there may also be other investigations, reports and surveying and engineering work required for acquiring all base data necessary to design a subdivision.

# CHAPTER 8

## SUBDIVISION DESIGN

### OVERVIEW

This chapter discusses the several steps that the surveying and engineering consultants will need to pursue to create a final subdivision design and development plans for a subdivision application.

Generally, there are multiple layouts of properties to be considered, unless the property is small or the terrain is restrictive, especially with respect to road layout, often the main control as to lot layout.

The Existing Conditions Plan is used to generate potential layouts of roads and lots. When one is selected, it will become a preliminary subdivision layout, and with refinement become the final subdivision plan.

## PRELIMINARY SUBDIVISION

**Preliminary subdivision layouts provide design options on:**

A.) Maximum lot yield
B.) Minimal road length and storm water drainage
C.) Minimizes wetlands impacts (when present)
D.) Minimal road cuts and fills
E.) Meets or exceeds open space requirements
F.) Minimizes blasting of ledge for road/storm water drainage by modifying its location when feasible

If you suspect a proposed road may have extensive areas of ledge, testing for its presence and its depth below existing terrain is prudent, as it provides your engineer the ability to possibly modify the design to decrease ledge involvement and construction costs.

By arriving at the subdivision design that meets as many of the above criteria as possible, you have the most effective subdivision design and potential to maximize profits.

If the subdivision is to be served by a public sewage sewer system, then individual lot soils investigations is not necessary. However, if the subdivision is to be served by individual, on-site subsurface sewage disposal systems, then each lot requires soil testing.

Proceeding with the final subdivision design before finalizing all lot soils testing runs the risk that the lot layout, road location and storm water drainage may need to be modified.

If you are also the homebuilder, you may want to investigate proposed house locations for the presence of, and depth to ledge, this will refine you estimate of lot development costs.

## MAXIMUM LOT YIELD VS. MINIMUM INFRASTRUCTURE COSTS

A crucial matter affecting the profitability of subdivisions is, the "yin and yang" between maximum lot yield and minimizing infrastructure construction costs. The major factor with respect to the above statement affecting a subdivisions profitability is whether the developer only sells lots or will also be the exclusive homebuilder for the subdivision.

**LOT YIELD**

**INFRASTRUCTURE COSTS**

A developer's maxim is: **"seek the maximum lot yield."** Why? As logically it should result in the greatest profit. Right? Let's discuss that maxim.

If only developing lots, look at whether areas of the subdivision have significantly higher Infrastructure cost and lower sales appeal. That could be an indicator that the profit from those lots could be significantly lower with respect to the return on investment desired.

This is particularly of concern when extensive blasting of ledge for road construction is necessary and/or very significant lengths of road must be constructed past undevelopable portions of the subdivision, such as open space reserves, to reach a relatively small developable area of the subdivision having limited lot yield. It may be best to combine these lots into large lots and market them as, "estates," "equestrian," or "farm lots."

The opposite rationale is of a developer who will also build the houses on all lots. If some lots in the subdivision won't generate much profit or are break-even with respect to development costs, there still is the profit from building the house. This developer always seeks maximum lot yield.

Also, as house construction costs are independent of infrastructure costs, most developers who are also the homebuilder will focus on building the highest dollar value homes the area will support, maximizing the profit from house construction, which further makes the case for seeking maximum lot yield when also building the homes.

Strictly from the point of view of maximizing profits, if you begin your developer career by subdividing lots, consider expansion into building houses in future subdivisions. Start by building houses towards the end of the subdivision when your development expenses are little or non-existent, your capital investment has been recovered and you have the profits from sold lots to fund homebuilding.

## SUBDIVISION PLANS

### OVERVIEW

Once a preliminary subdivision layout has been selected, the work then commences on finalizing the lot and road layout, generating lots that accurately meet all zoning, subdivsion, inland wetlands, and health department regulations. The Existing Conditions Plan discussed in Chapter 7 contains the majority of the precise base information needed to convert the preliminary subdivision layout into the various subdivision plans. Using both the preliminary subdivision layout and the existing conditions plan, the geometry of the lots, road right-of-ways, easements, and open space areas are determined and coupled with engineering designs of roads, storm water drainage system, and design detais for other infrastructure construction, the subdivision is can be finalized.

### THE SUBDIVISION PACKAGE – CONSISTS OF

**Subdivision Plans:**

A.) Subdivision Map
B.) Wetlands Boundary Map
C.) Site Development Plan
D.) Road Construction Plan and Profile
E.) Inland Wetlands Regulated Activity Plan
F.) Construction Detail Plans

**Plans Possibly Required:**

A.) Post Development Storm Water Detention/Retention Plan
B.) Offsite Improvements Construction Plan

C.) Environmental/Wetlands Mitigation Plan
D.) Other plans, either per regulations or unique to the subdivision.
E.) Archeological and Protected Features Plan or Report
F.) As-built Road and Storm Drainage Plan

## OTHER TYPES OF RESIDENTIAL SUBDIVISIONS

The regulatory standards of a municipality, or other political jurisdiction for residential subdivisions is often limited to a single concept where the area, width, depth, geometric shape, etc. of a lot is the only difference between the zoning districts. The typical subdivisions of the past several decades throughout much of the U.S. are the result of this concept.

However, there are several alternate types of subdivisions whose regulations and standards seek to create a different living environment. If you are interested in exploring possible options to a "standard" subdivision you will need to review the zoning and subdivision regulations to determine if any of the following have been adopted. Each has a significantly different purpose from a "standard" subdivision and dissimilar design regulations.

**"Open Space Development Subdivision."** I personally favor this type subdivision as it generally provides the same lot yield as a standard subdivision with the bonus of lower development costs and preserving a massive open space. Guilford requires a minimum of 50% of the property with lot yield almost always maintained versus a standard subdivision which only requires 10% open space. For more information see, **"Chapter 8 – Subdivision Design, Open Space Development Subdivisions"** for a detailed discussion. In some jurisdictions it may be known as a "cluster" subdivision or by another name.

**"Mixed Use Subdivision."** A little used type of subdivision, certainly the case in Connecticut, but which I think has exciting potential, explore it in your area. This type of subdivision combines in the same two-story condominium unit a residential use on the upper floor and on the ground floor a nonresidential work area limited by zoning to uses such as, a professional office, art studio, or a craft retail business. Both floors must be occupied by the same owner.

**"Equestrian Subdivisions."** Certainly not common in Connecticut, my practice only developed one. It was a high-end facility situated midway between Boston and Manhattan meant for the affluent equestrian as an extended getaway, not as the primary year-round residence though the proposed homes were quite substantial. The buyers were offered a custom architect designed home with substantial equestrian facilities such as, extensive riding trails, numerous paddocks, a professionally staffed stable for the owner's horses located on common land, and an individual connecting riding trail from an optional one or two horse shed located on a lot to the main riding trail system.

**"Farm Subdivisions."** A more appropriate name would be a gentlemen's farm. The purpose was to reduce excessive numbers and/or types of animals being kept in the backyards of residential subdivision homes and complaints from the neighbors. It typically required a minimum of five acres, thereby permitting more types of livestock and in greater numbers.

**"Accessory Apartment Subdivisions."** In Connecticut, an accessory apartment was not actually a type of subdivision but where an apartment could either be attached to a home or be a detached structure. They were individually approved by a special permit application process requiring a public hearing. There were several restrictions of which the main ones were, only being applicable to an existing home, limited square footage, the occupants had to be immediate family such as elderly parents, and often no separate kitchen could be included. I would like to think that a more creative (compassionate) municipality might allow them for new home subdivisions, with so many people living many years longer, check the municipal zoning regulations, it could be quite viable in certain markets.

## OPEN SPACE DEVELOPMENT SUBDIVISIONS

### OVERVIEW

The goal of an Open Space Development Subdivision is to leave a significant percentage of the property's area undisturbed to maintain the existing habitat upon the property. This larger open space is created by reducing the area permitted for development. While this sounds like a negative for you the developer, as less development area equates to fewer lots, in the spirit of that old phrase, "it ain't necessarily so," if the regulations are crafted to maintain the lot yield. To that goal, maintaining the same lot yield, a unique set of zoning and subdivision regulations need to be in effect, and generally are referred to as the "open space development subdivision method."

**Open Space Development Subdivision versus a standard subdivision – the same lot yield**

**How? With these key zoning standard modifications:**

A.) Decreasing the minimum lot area

B.) Decreasing the minimum lot frontage

C.) Decreasing the geometric shape within the lot (if any) to be compatible with 'A' and 'B' above

D.) Decreasing the lot minimum buildable area (if any) to be compatible with 'A' and 'B' above

E.) Modify/eliminate other zoning standards to accomplish the intent of this development method

Other regulations still must be met on the reduced area open space subdivision lots, the two principal ones being the ability of each lot to support an on-site subsurface sewage disposal system and a 100% reserve area if no public sewage sewer system is available, and/or an on-site well if no public water supply is available.

This development method by using a smaller portion of the property also reduces road length which lowers construction costs for the developer and maintenance costs for the municipality. How's that sound?

To determine the maximum lot yield for an Open Space Development Subdivision, the same technical data which is required for a "standard subdivision" is necessary. A boundary survey and map, wetlands boundary map (if present), and the topography of the property.

**Methods to Determine Maximum Lot Yield of an Open Space Subdivision:**

A.) The lot yield from a preliminary standard subdivision layout

**OR**

B.) Deduct from the total property area regulation specified types of land, such as, wetlands, steep slopes, ledge outcrops, proposed roads, etc., and then divide the remaining area by a regulation specified factor to determine the maximum lot yield

**OR**

C.) Deduct a regulation specified percentage of the property which must be designated as open with the remaining area being divided by a regulation specified factor to determine the maximum lot yield

The lot yield determined by one of the above methods sets the maximum lot yield for an Open Space Development Subdivision, however the maximum lot yield can only be obtained if the lots also meet all the zoning, subdivision, and public health standards as specified for this method of subdivision development.

**Road standards may also be modified, lowering road construction costs, such as**:

A.) Where appropriate, no curbs with roads draining by sheet flow off the road onto adjoining land, eliminating much of, or all of, a storm water drainage system

B.) Permanent cul-de-sac roads with low traffic volume may have reduced standards for pavement width, road subbase depth, and pavement thickness

Finally, Guilford from the beginning of the regulation to encourage developers to commit to an open space development subdivision when they were not mandatory, bonus lots potentially could be obtained. They were granted in addition to the maximum number of lots determined by one of the lot yield calculations, if the increased lot yield did not decrease the minimum required open space area and all lots met the public health code standards. It was eliminated after several years as an inducement as developers flocked to this type of development, eventually it became the mandatory subdivision design with an occasional property excepted.

# CHAPTER 9

## REGULATORY AGENCIES

## AGENCIES, APPLICATIONS, PRESENTATIONS, PUBLIC HEARINGS

### OVERVIEW

This chapter discuss several regulatory matters involved in the: preparation of; presentation of; response to unfavorable actors and actions, and defense of your application for subdivision when denied or burdened with unacceptable conditions of approval.

## AGENCIES

**Regulatory Agencies with Subdivision Jurisdiction**

A.) Planning and Zoning Commission (if separate commissions, generally the planning commission)
B.) Wetlands Commission
C.) Conservation Commission, a.k.a. Environmental Commission|
D.) Historic District and Properties Commission
E.) Water Pollution Control Authority (connecting to public sewage system)
F.) Municipal Advisory Agencies
G.) Fire Services
H.) Water Authority (potable water supply)
I.) Aquifer Protection Agency
J.) State Department of Environmental Protection (D.E.P.)
K.) State Department of Health (subsurface sewage disposal system)
L.) State Highway Department (connecting subdivision road or drainage to state facilities)

## APPLICATIONS

A.) Planning and Zoning Commission – subdivision
B.) Inland Wetlands Commission – wetlands boundary delineation

C.) Inland Wetlands Commission – regulated activity permit
D.) Health Department – sewage disposal system plan (individual lots)
E.) Engineering Department – (road and storm water drainage design and post development control)
F.) State Highway Department – to connect to a state road and/or facilities

If utilities such as, water, electricity, and sewer system are provided by the municipality, agreement with each municipal utility will probably be required either before or concurrently with the subdivision application, or subsequently to subdivision approval but prior to commencing infrastructure construction.

The responsibility for completing all required applications should be that of your consultants, your function is to come up with the name of the subdivision, road names, sign the applications, and write the application fee checks. Once you have developed several subdivisions you will have gained the expertise to complete all, or many portions of the applications.

## APPLICATION PRESENTATION

Some of the regulatory agencies mentioned at the beginning of the chapter may only review plans without requiring an applicant presentation to obtain their approval. Presentation of applications before the Planning and Zoning and Inland Wetland Commissions however, will need to be made by one or more of your consultants who designed the subdivision, and if necessary, by your attorney.

It has been a team effort up to this point, with the land surveyor or engineer as the project manager, coordinating the work of the other consultants, but now the game plan requires selection of whom will be the lead presenter of applications before each regulatory agency.

### Planning and Zoning Commission

If a specific issue is believed to be of concern to the commission, it should be the initial matter addressed by the appropriate consultant, as acting early and forthright may alleviate commission members concerns and reduce the number of questions they ask. If there is no specific issue, then either the land surveyor or engineer is the appropriate choice as the lead presenter.

### Inland Wetlands Commission

**Boundary** – The inland wetland boundary application is presented by either the land surveyor or the soil scientist. At times certain wetlands may have reports including unique soils profiles, for those applications the soil scientist should be the presenter.

**Regulated Activity** – If regulated activities are proposed within inland wetlands and/or regulated uplands, the commission's approval is key to also obtaining subdivision approval by the Planning and Zoning Commission. It is important that either your consultant soil scientist or environmentalist and engineer be the presenters in addition to having guided the commission on their field inspection to the regulated activity areas.

If subsurface sewage disposal systems for individual lots in the subdivision are within a regulated area or area of concern, it must be demonstrated how the proposed system design eliminates bacteria and nutrients from reaching and contaminating the wetlands, it should be presented by the engineer for the subdivision.

Be aware that the Inland Wetlands Commission's regulated activity regulations may have sufficient "gray area" language allowing the commission to require additional investigation or plan design.

### Concerns - Planning and Zoning and Inland Wetland Commissions

If it is believed that a commission or a member may be pre-disposed negatively towards your application, your attorney should be the lead presenter. When an attorney is the lead presenter it may result in the commission or member being more cautious.

Attorneys can subtly or directly remind members of a commission that if an application is in conformance with regulations, the commission (especially the P&Z commission) is obligated to approve it, otherwise it is effectively an uncompensated taking, a violation of state statutes and/or case law.

While members of the team are presenting an application and a member presents a less than neutral attitude, it should be made obvious to the commission members that your attorney is busily taking notes. It conveys the message that unjustified actions by a member, or the commission would be challenged in court. Commissions are aware that the town father's ire will be felt for legal bills to defend an appeal of a frivolous decision by a commission.

## PUBLIC HEARINGS

Regulatory hearings for presentation of applications for subdivision before the Planning and Zoning Commission, and the Inland Wetlands Commission, can either be a regular meeting or a public hearing held specifically for the application. Which type meeting is held is either dictated by regulations or is per the decision of the commission if it feels the application will be of significant public interest and believe it appropriate to provide the public the opportunity to formally comment, question, be supportive, or express opposition. It also will provide the most comprehensive record of the application hearing, beneficial to all parties if an appeal of the decision of the commission is initiated.

The applicant is responsible in meeting the statutory requirements which enable a public hearing to commence, failure to meet all criteria will result in postponement of the public hearing until the applicant corrects the omission in a timely manner, failure to do so, will result in terminating future consideration of the application, necessitating submittal of a new application.

Using Connecticut as an example, public hearings require specific notice to both property owners adjoining and/or within a specified distance from the subject property, and to the general population of the municipality.

A.) Legal Notice – published in a local newspaper to inform residents of the application

B.) Legal Notice – notice of application also sent by certified or return notice U.S. mail to owners whose property either adjoins or is within a specified distance of the subject property

C.) Signage on property – notice of the public hearing.

The above notices have specific time frames to be placed prior to the public hearing date. Public Hearings must also commence on the stated date, time and location specified in the legal notice. If any regular business of the commission is being heard before the public hearing start time, it must be tabled and either continued after the conclusion of the public hearing or to a future meeting so the public hearing can commence at its legally specified time.

**Sequence Format of a Public Hearing (Connecticut):**

A.) Chairperson announces the public hearing is commencing (at time per legal notice)

B.) Chairperson verifies a quorum is present and introduces the members of the commission

C.) Chairperson explains the procedures of a public hearing to the attendees

D.) The commission chairperson or secretary reads the public hearing legal notice

E.) Applicant begins presentation of their application

F.) Commission members may ask questions during and/or after the applicant's presentation

G.) Chairperson or a commission member reads for the record, reports of staff, and all correspondence

H.) The chairperson offers the public that have **comments or questions** the opportunity to speak

I.) The commission may answer the public comments or questions, or request the applicant to do so

J.) The commission offers the public **in favor** of the application the opportunity to speak

K.) The commission offers the public **in opposition** to the application the opportunity to speak

L.) The commission may or may not choose to respond to an opposition statement.

M.) The chairperson offers the applicant the opportunity to rebut opposition statements

At this time the chairperson will confer with the other members as to whether additional information is required from the applicant and/or additional time is needed to provide those attendees in opposition not able to speak because of the approaching end to the allotted meeting time. If either is in the affirmative, the meeting will not be closed but continued to the next scheduled commission meeting date. Even it the commission has no request for additional information from the applicant, the applicant may want to introduce additional information and may request a continuation of the public hearing.

If it is determined that there is no need to continue the hearing to the next meeting, the chairperson will make a motion to close the public hearing per one of the following:

A.) Close the public hearing and take no further action until the next meeting

B.) Close the public hearing, discuss the application and continue further action until the next meeting

C.) Close the public hearing, discuss the application and then vote whether to approve or deny.

Voting on the application must take place within the state statutory period for a decision. Upon voting, the commission shall publish a legal notice as to its decision on the application.

# ADJOINING PROPERTY OWNERS

Every proposed subdivision has adjoining properties, mostly privately owned. As a developer you have a decision to make with respect to those adjoining properties that have homes upon them.

Which is, should you proactively seek to meet with these owners to introduce yourself and inform them about your proposed subdivision, or do the alternative, avoid initiating contact.

My developer clients who also were building homes were more likely to approach adjoining owners while those developing lots for sale were less likely to contact the owners.

So, where does this leave a first-time developer who likely is only developing lots, not building? If the property is in the town where you reside, and you are known in town, I believe speaking with the adjoining property owners is the best option. If you do not reside in town or are a very recent arrival probably not.

If you decide to approach owners, then approach all of them, do not leave anyone out, otherwise those owners may think you are hiding something from them. Also, do not agree to accept an offer by an owner to speak on your behalf to other owners, as that may result in misunderstood information being communicated, potentially worse than no communication.

After you have spoken with the adjoining owners, should you or should you not ask them to support your project? If you believe that you and your project have been well received, then probably yes, but only if you think their support is necessary for the success of your subdivision application and generally at a subsequent not the initial meeting.

Any request for support should be made after the initial meeting, otherwise you will come across as just interested in yourself. If asking for support, have a brief typewritten letter for their consideration, with a stamped envelope addressed to the Planning and Zoning Commission chairperson. Also, let them know it is okay for them to submit their own letter.

# OPPOSITION BY ADJOINING OWNERS AND INTERVENORS

## ADJOINING OWNERS – Supportive, Disinterested, Hostile.

Some owners are reasonable in opposition, seeking minor plan modifications adjacent to their property. While other owners who are unhappy about a proposed subdivision adjoining them, the **"not in my backyard"** folks may be a problem for you.

A potential always exists for those in opposition to take different degrees of opposition, such as:

A.) Informal neighborhood group appearing en masse at application hearings in opposition

B.) An attorney, engineer or soil scientist hired by an inf\dividual or group to oppose the application

C.) Contacting the local newspaper as to why the application should be denied

Your attorney may or may not advise you to meet with neighborhood opposition to see if their concerns can be resolved; however, the Planning and Zoning Commission may also encourage the applicant and opposition to meet and try to seek resolution prior to subsequent commission meetings.

Affluent adjoining owners can be aggressive in their opposition, funding besides an attorney land use professionals to review the subdivision plans and documents looking for anything, no matter how marginal, that they will attempt to magnify as a reason for the commission to deny the application. Owners of this persuasion have the goal to stop you permanently. They are not interested in modifications to the plan, they seek denial of the application. If not denied, their next strategy could be to tie you up with legal appeals, the hope being that the cost and time involved will end your interest in continuing your application.

Legal appeal of an approved subdivision is a suit against the approving commission the Planning and Zoning Commission. There is potentially particularly good news though. Courts generally decide in favor of the Planning and Zoning Commission as they are seen as acting in the best interest of the municipality as a whole, not a very small group of individuals.

The resultant if your application approval is appealed is that you have time delays and legal costs, but your project ends up being highly likely able to proceed to completion.

## INTERVENORS

Additionally, intervenors if permitted by the laws of your state, may enter the fray against you. Intervenors are individuals or organizations with the purpose, "to intervene for the public good" in land use applications. Intervenors, particularly organizations, are well versed in land use matters, state statutes and case law, and are generally funded sufficiently to be a potentially serious opposition. Intervenor involvement immediately calls for your attorney's participation. Intervenors, if unsuccessful in persuading a commission to deny an application, may proceed with a lawsuit. The good news is that intervenors focus on applications with allegedly significant impact on the environment, not a run-of-the mill residential subdivision.

## CONDITIONS OF APPROVAL

Subdivision maps and associated plans are often modified during the application process by the applicant in response to comments of one or more of the regulatory commissions or their staff. In addition to the possibility of modifications during the application presentation process, a motion to approve an application may have conditions to the approval which shall require plan modification prior to being able to file the map and or plans in the land record'.

### Conditions of Approval May Include the Following:

A.) Beginning date to commence infrastructure construction
B.) Seasonal limits on infrastructure construction
C.) Method of conveying open space
D.) Is access to open space: seasonally limited; open to the public or closed to protect unique species
E.) Home building permits not issued until road binder pavement course installed
F.) Home building permits not issued until fire protection is operational
G.) Lots served by wells, no issuance of house building permit until a drilled well is approved.

The conditions of approval specific to the subdivision map or other design plans will need to be made before the subdivision map will be signed by the chairperson of the Planning and Zoning Commission, a requirement for its filing in the land records of the Town Clerk per commission regulations and state statutes.

## APPLICATION ACTIONS

### Planning and Zoning Commission Subdivision Application:

A.) If the application is determined to be complete, it may proceed
B.) Applications determined to be incomplete, cannot proceed.

An application deemed to be complete is a request for action on the application by the regulatory agency, whose action can be:

A.) To approve as submitted
B.) To approve with conditions of the agency
C.) To deny without prejudice
D.) To deny with prejudice

Denial of an application without prejudice allows the applicant to submit a new application as soon as the concerns of the agency have been addressed with plan modifications. A denial with prejudice means that the application is either seriously lacking in compliance with regulations or that the concept of development was unacceptable, the applicant may not be able to submit a new application for a specified period of time, and the application must be substantially different than the one denied.

**Do not get nervous after reading the above.** The reality is that from my professional experience presenting applications is that "to deny with prejudice" is very uncommon. Also, "to deny without prejudice" is generally easily corrected, getting your revised application quickly back before the commission.

Finally, "to approve with conditions" is quite common, many conditions can be seen to be coming based upon commission questions and comments during the hearing(s).

## APPEAL OF APPROVED OR DENIED APPLICATION

A subdivision application is a request to approve it, the commission may approve it as submitted, or approve it with conditions, or deny it.

Subsequent, to action by a regulatory agency and its notice of its decision to the public, a statutory period begins for an allegedly aggrieved party to file a lawsuit appealing the agency decision. Lawsuits are almost always by adjoining property owners, very occasionally by a regulatory agency, the applicant, or an intervenor.

Applicants generally appeal a denied application, however on very rare occasions the applicant may appeal an application approval if it included either a condition of approval that the applicant viewed as extremely burdensome or was believed to be outside of the commission's authority to impose.

Third parties, whether an individual, an informal group of neighborhood property owners, or an intervenor, would only be appealing an approval of a subdivision application.

Another municipal regulatory agency could appeal an application approved by the Planning and Zoning Commission. It is extremely uncommon, but if a regulatory agency believes the approved plan has negative impacts upon areas of its regulatory responsibility, it could feel it is obligated to do so.

The Inland Wetlands Commission is the likely agency to object to a Planning and Zoning Commission approval, due to construction within wetlands or the adjacent regulated uplands. The most common objections of the wetlands agency involve, roads, driveways, placement of fill, and subsurface sewage disposal systems, when it believes alternatives exist to moderate or eliminate impacts on the wetlands.

Some Planning and Zoning and Inland Wetlands Commissions to minimize conflicts resulting from their respective actions on applications, have appointed a member of their commission to the other commission as a non-voting communicator during the application hearing process.

**NOTE:** An appeal stays the start of the statutory period for filing an approved subdivision map.

# CHAPTER 10

## ADVISORY AGENCY & NON-REGULATORY ORGANIZATIONS

### OVERVIEW

**Advisory agencies** of a municipality have as their purpose proffering comments and recommendations regarding a defined area of responsibility that a regulatory commission must consider as part of its review and decision process on applications.

**Non-regulatory organizations** are independent of municipal control, their objective being the protection and enhancement of lands within the municipality for the benefit of its residents, wildlife, and fauna.

## ADVISORY AGENCIES

Some municipalities land use regulations for subdivision applications require input from one or more advisory agencies to the Planning and Zoning (P&Z) Commission either during the staff process of reviewing applications and/or during commission meetings on an application.

The purpose of an advisory agency is to provide comments specific to its charge area on a submitted subdivision application. The most common advisory agency I have occasionally encountered in my Connecticut consultant subdivision practice is the Conservation Agency, though in other jurisdictions it may have another name, or have a formal application hearing process.

Advisory agencies were not common in the municipalities where I practiced, they received application information directly from the P&Z staff not the applicant, with their comments on an application directed to the commission not the applicant, having no direct interaction with the advisory agency.

The comments of advisory agencies I experienced were not mandatory for adoption or implementation by the P&Z commission when considering its decision on a subdivision application, as the name implies their comments are advisory.

However, for a municipality with advisory agencies where you propose to develop, prudence dictates a check to determine if they have any regulatory authority.

## NON-REGULATORY ORGANIZATIONS

Most municipalities have organizations which are entirely or partially focused on land preservation, its use, public access, and education on the benefits of its preservation, but have no regulatory authority.

Land preservation trusts strength comes from its membership, which can be local, regional, statewide, or national. Local trusts of each municipality are almost exclusively who is involved in applications that require preservation of portions of a property as open space. They are respected and listened to, by the land use agencies as these are their fellow citizens.

**Typical Land Preservation Organizations:**

| | |
|---|---|
| **Local** | Historical Society<br>Land Preservation Trust<br>Sports Associations<br>Hiking and horse trail development advocates |
| **Statewide** | Historical Society<br>Hiking and horse trail preservation and development advocates<br>Advocates for public access to, and conversion of, abandoned rail and trolley lines, and canal towpaths for walking, biking, horseback riding, and similar uses |
| **National** | Sierra Club<br>Ducks Unlimited<br>National Wildlife Federation<br>Audubon Society |

Of these organizations, the local land preservation trust generally is the entity most interested in accepting land being dedicated as open space, a requirement of the subdivision regulations. However, if there is a unique aspect to the proposed open space parcel, one of the other entities may be a better steward.

Whether it is the local land preservation trust or one of the other entities you need to approach them to offer the proposed open space parcel many weeks prior to submitting a subdivision application. This gives the organization the time to physically inspect the property as to its suitability with respect to the purpose of the organization, followed by a meeting to discuss the property, and if there is a consensus to accept it, extending a written offer of their interest in accepting the open space.

Once you have an organization prepared to accept the open space, ask if a representative of the organization would be willing to attend the Planning and Zoning Commission meeting to address why their organization is interested in obtaining the open space, and how it will benefit the municipality. Obviously, for the preservation trust to receive the open space the commission needs to approve your application for subdivision, they won't miss the connection.

The one organization you should avoid approaching for general support is the Economic Development Commission, their focus is on commercial not residential development, commissions considering residential subdivision applications do not appreciate their appearance nor input.

# CHAPTER 11

## CLOSING AND POST CLOSING

### OVERVIEW

The last step in purchasing real estate is known as the closing. Closings are performed by attorneys in Connecticut, in other states it can be by either an attorney, a title closer or title agent. This chapter discusses those matters which must be addressed per Connecticut practice and specific regulations of regulatory agencies with respect to their approval of subdivisions. Some closing matters are addressed at the closing, or prior to closing or post-closing. Verify with your attorney the requirements of your state and regulatory agencies of the municipality where your property is located.

## DEADLINE TO FILE APPROVED SUBDIVISION

When a subdivision is approved, the subdivision map must be filed in the land records of the municipality within the time frame specified in the State statutes.

The subdivision regulations or the policy of the Planning and Zoning Commission (P&Z) may require other maps and plans associated with the approved subdivision to also be filed, such as: the property survey map; site plan(s); road/storm drainage construction plans, and possibly other designated plans.

The start date to record the approved subdivision map begins upon publication of a legal notice of its approval in a local newspaper and/or the P&Z website. The start date to record a subdivision map will be postponed if an appeal challenging its approval is filed within the statutory period to file with Superior Court.

Deadline to file an appealed subdivision approval begins upon whichever concludes the appeal:

A.) Dismissal/denial of the lawsuit by Superior Court
B.) Denial of an appeal of its decision by said court

C.) Denial of an appeal of the Superior Court decision by the Appellate Court
D.) Denial of an appeal of its decision by said court
E.) Denial of a petition to the Supreme Court to hear an appeal of the Appellate Court denial
F.) Denial of an appeal to the Supreme Court of the Appellate Court denial
G.) Withdrawal of the lawsuit at any time by the plaintiff at any stage of appeal

Connecticut state statutes and the municipal subdivision regulations require that an approved subdivision map must be recorded in the land records within 90 days of publication of a legal notice of the approval of the subdivision, or within 90 days from the conclusion of an appeal of said approval.

Prior to the end of the deadline period to record a subdivision map in Connecticut, the applicant may request that the P&Z Commission consider an extension of 90 days to record the map in the land records. If an extension is granted, before its end date an additional 90-day extension may be requested. If it is granted, a final 90-day extension may be granted if requested prior to the expiration of the second 90-day extension. If all extensions are granted, recordation of a subdivision map can be postponed for a total of 270 days.

**NOTE:** Failure of the applicant to file the subdivision map in the land records before the end of whichever of the above deadline situations governs, will result in the approval of the subdivision becoming null and void, ending its ability to be filed in the land records. The subdivision would then revert to its prior condition, a tract of undeveloped land. Any future subdivision of the land would require a new subdivision application conforming to the regulations then in effect and repeating the entire application process.

Effect upon approved wetlands maps or plans when an approved subdivision map becomes null and void:

A.) Wetlands Boundary Map – no effect on ability to file said map
B.) Regulated Activity Plans – approval is meaningless without a filed subdivision map. If the same subdivision map and plans are approved by P&Z in a new application and filed in the land records, state statutes and/or the municipal wetlands regulations will dictate if the earlier approved plan(s) are still valid, or that they also need to again go through the application approval process. This is a question to refer to your attorney.

## BONDING

When P&Z approves a subdivision with infrastructure improvements, regulations require that the developer post a performance bond. The purpose of a performance bond is to assure funds are available for the municipality to complete installation of remaining infrastructure when a developer has financially failed or abandoned the project.

However, the municipality would only call the bond to complete remaining infrastructure if one or more lots or homes in the subdivision had been sold to third parties, and only if said properties are located on an uncompleted subdivision road. If all lots or homes sold are on a completed subdivision road or an existing public road the bond would not be called as municipalities would not be obligated to build out the remainder of a failed subdivision.

The posting of a performance bond will be required either before the subdivision map can be signed by the chairperson of the Planning and Zoning (P&Z) Commission for filing in the land records of the municipality, or prior to commencement of infrastructure construction.

**Performance bond type and amount will be specified by the P&Z Commission.**

A.) Letter of credit issued by a bank
B.) Surety bond
C.) Cash deposited by the developer in a joint bank account of the developer and municipality

The bond amount is identical for all three types of bonding. Connecticut municipalities have pretty much moved to cash bonds deposited with a bank, as it eliminates potential disputes with either the issuer of a letter of credit, or of a surety bond, to fulfill their obligation without the municipality having to resort to lengthy negotiations or legal action.

At appropriate intervals as portions of the subdivision infrastructure are completed and have been approved by an inspector for the municipality, and the developers engineer or construction management consultant concur, the developer may request the commission to approve release a portion of the performance bond equivalent to the value of the installed improvements. This may be repeated numerous times for subdivisions with extensive infrastructure.

Upon final completion of all infrastructure improvements which shall become the property and maintenance responsibility of the municipality, the developer can request both the acceptance of all improvements by the municipality and the release of the balance of the performance bond.

Other municipal agencies may also have bonding requirements, in particular the Inland Wetlands Commission (IWC) to address any environmental impacts due to construction, within wetlands or in proximity to them. Partial release of bonding may also be permitted by the IWC regulations.

For more on performance bonds refer to, "Chapter 14 – Infrastructure Construction, Performance Bonds" and for maintenance bonding refer to, "Chapter 15 – Infrastructure Post Construction, Maintenance Bond Posting and Release".

If off-site improvements are also required on non-municipal roads, such as a state highway, posting of a performance bond and liability insurance will be required prior to the issuance of a construction permit. Anticipate that no partial bond releases will be considered.

## APPROVAL OF LEGAL DOCUMENTS

There are certain documents that are required to be recorded in the municipal land records concurrently with the approved subdivision map. Those documents which convey either a fee interest, a right, an easement, or impose a restriction of use upon a portion of the subdivision property, in favor of the municipality, will almost assuredly require review of said documents and approval by the legal consul either of the Planning and Zoning Commission, or of the municipality.

**Some Possible Documents:**

A.) Fee or Easement – For sewage pump stations; fire water storage tanks or ponds; open space, etc.

B.) Right to Maintain – Removal of obstructions on individual lots and homeowner association property such as, that which obstructs the sight line of a road

C.) Restrictive Easement – Prohibiting lot owners or the public from either accessing the area of the subdivision subject to the easement or restricting specific activity within it.

The deed for subdivision road(s) depending upon policy, may either be reviewed and approved prior to recording the approved subdivision map, or prior to commencement of construction, or prior to the developer requesting acceptance of the completed road(s) by the municipality.

## MARKETABLE TITLE – FINAL UPDATE

### OVERVIEW

Determination of the Marketability of Title, whether for purchasing a home, a building lot, a parcel of land, or an approved subdivision, normally is performed several days prior to the scheduled closing. Its purpose is to ascertain that the real estate you are purchasing has both a clear chain of title and that there are no encumbrances affecting it. It will be based upon a search of the municipalities Town Clerk's land records and the Tax Collector's records.

**Definitions:**

**Chain of Title** – The recorded history of the ownership of a property from the present owner, searching back a specified number of year either per the General Statutes of your State, or per the established practice of the legal profession for the locality of the property, or per title insurance company requirements.

This search besides determining if there are any irregularities in the grantor/grantee sequence of prior transfers of the property, "the deed chain", or if a description of the property in a deed isn't in conformance with the current deed or other prior deed descriptions, excepting for; a conveyance of a portion of the property out of the property; or conveyance of land into the property.

If the property being conveyed has a property survey performed as part of its subdivision, a new deed for its conveyance will be written based upon this property survey map, superseding all prior deed descriptions.

**Encumbrances:**

Grant of Right – A party other than the owner having a right, such as, but not limited to, leases, easements, or an option to purchase the property.

Financial Obligation – Owner debt, such as, but not limited to, mortgages, property taxes due, tax lien (municipal, state, federal), or a mechanics lien.

Legal Notice – Owner subject to final or ongoing legal actions, such as, but not limited to:

A.) Judgment of a court
B.) Third party claim of title interest
C.) Foreclosure Notice of property
D.) Bankruptcy Notice
E.) Claim of adverse possession
F.) Suit regarding property boundary location

If a problem is discovered and the seller can resolve it quickly, the closing likely will proceed. However, if it is not resolvable, or not resolvable in a reasonable amount of time, or the seller chooses not to attempt to resolve it, the buyer would be entitled to void the contract and receive back all deposit monies.

For a buyer of a home, building lot, or a small parcel of land, upon the return of deposit monies the buyer's loss is primarily limited to the time spent in searching for the property. However, the inability to close on an approved subdivision, even with the return of deposit monies, will result in substantial buyer financial loss due to the significant expenses in obtaining approval of a subdivision.

To minimize the possibility of such an outcome, the developer should implement the actions discussed in, "Chapter 1 – Seeking A Property, Preliminary Due Diligence – Prior To Contract Submittal". The investigations recommended therein will be key in determining whether to move forward, or not, with an offer to purchase, thereby likely avoiding the problems cited above and the financial loose.

If an offer to purchase is submitted and results in a successful closing, the buyer should receive a full reimbursement by the seller to make whole the buyer's expense for the initial due diligence marketable title investigation, as it replaced the majority of what is typically done just before the closing. Include it as a contract condition.

## CLOSING

### OVERVIEW

The closing is the last step in obtaining complete control of your subdivision after obtaining all its necessary approvals, now its ownership can be transferred to you.

However, there are several important aspects of the closing that first must be addressed before setting the closing date.

**Prior to Closing – Attorney Review of Applicable Documents:**

A.) Regulatory agencies letters of approval signed by the chairperson or other authorized individual

B.) Maps and plans required to be filed in the land records, signed by the chairperson of the agency

C.) Marketable Title – Final Update

D.) Release of seller from any mortgage or lien, if payment due, paid before or at the closing.

E.) Release of any third-party rights or leases that can be terminated by seller.

F.) Lender purchase commitment letter for buyer financing.

G.) Lender purchase mortgage deed and promissory note

H.) Lender construction loan commitment, financing documents, and availability of funds
I.) Certificate of Title from seller
J.) Liability insurance coverage effective as of the closing date
K.) Title insurance policy, effective as of the closing date.
L.) Warranty Deed with its description based upon the property survey map prepared by the subdivision land surveyor
M.) Deeding of any portion of the subdivision if required, concurrently with your closing, such as, open space or land along an existing public road to create a uniform road right-of-way width.

During the closing all applicable documents will again be reviewed by your attorney with you, and that documents being received by you or that you are executing will be signed by the appropriate party, you, the seller, or your lender. Also, that all funds necessary to pay the seller are in hand, and that any financial obligations of the seller are paid.

**Title Insurance Policy.** An extremely important safeguard, providing protection against claims by third parties as to having a fee interest in the property or having other rights. The policy provides for legal representation on behalf of you the buyer, to defend against said claims. Additionally, it will reimburse you the insured for financial loss up to the policy limit.

**NOTE:** Several items that if applicable, will either be part of the closing, or addressed post-closing, depending upon the requirements of the approving regulatory agencies:

A.) A performance bond for Planning and Zoning for subdivision infrastructure construction
B.) An environmental bond for the Wetlands Commission to restore damage to wetlands
C.) An environmental bond for Planning and Zoning to address any such damage
D.) A performance bond for any off-site municipal road improvements (may be included in 'A')
E.) Open space to be conveyed to a subdivision homeowners association or a non-profit land preservation organization

## OPEN SPACE

### OVERVIEW

Subdivisions in Connecticut are required to set aside a portion of the property for the preservation of the existing natural habitat of the property. These parcels of land are legally dedicated as permanent open space for the enhancement of the quality of life of the residents of the municipality.

**The Legal Components to Establish Open Space:**

A.) Entity agreeing to accept land
B.) Type of conveyance
C.) Access permitted by whom?
D.) Obligations of grantee

**Control or Ownership by:**

A.) State Forest – if open space can be attached to existing state forest land
B.) Land preservation trust based in the municipality where subdivision is located
C.) State, regional, or national land and wildlife preservation organizations
D.) Subdivision homeowner's association

**Type of Conveyance:**

A.) Warranty Deed – fee to property
B.) Easement – Upon portions of subdivision lots (easement area remains taxable)
C.) Conservation Restriction – Specifies either uses permitted or uses prohibited.

**Access Rights to Open Space:**

A.) General Public
B.) Restricted to owners in the subdivision
C.) Closed to all (generally to preserve endangered flora and/or fauna).

## DOCUMENTS RECORDED OR FILED POST CLOSING

### OVERVIEW

Once the closing is completed, certain documents must be recorded in the land records of the municipality where the subdivision is located, thereby protecting you the purchaser and the interests of any lender and satisfying the regulations of the regulatory agencies.

## DOCUMENTS RECORDED – IMMEDIATELY

### Developer Documents:

A.) Property Survey Map
B.) Division Map of Property (if subdivision is not of entire property)
C.) Subdivision Map
D.) Warranty Deed

### Lender Documents – Property Purchase:

A.) Promissory Note
B.) Mortgage Deed

## DOCUMENTS RECORDED – IMMEDIATELY OR SOON THEREAFTER

### Developer Documents:

A.) Inland Wetlands Boundary Map
B.) Subdivision Design Plans (if required by regulatory agency)
C.) Open Space Deed
D.) Easements (such as, storm water detention and retention areas; fire protection ponds or tanks)

### Lender Documents – Infrastructure Construction:

A.) Loan documents
B.) Performance Bond

## DOCUMENTS RECORDED – GENERALLY AT A FUTURE DATE

### Developer Documents:

A.) Utility easement maps
B.) Utility Easement deeds
C.) Declaration of Covenants and Restrictions
D.) Homeowners Association regulations

### Planning and Zoning Commission Documents:

A.) As-built plans of subdivision roads and storm drainage
B.) Deed to convey subdivision road right-of-way(s) to municipality
C.) An updated subdivision map of road and lot monumentation set (if required by regulations).

# DECLARATION OF COVENANTS AND RESTRICTIONS

## OVERVIEW

Covenants and Restrictions have two purposes, to protect the developer's substantial investment in creating a subdivision, and represent to potential buyers of lots or home/lot packages that the value of their investment will be protected. Covenants and Restrictions are created by the developer and then implemented by recordation in the land records prior to offering lots for sale or home/lot packages, providing buyers with full disclosure. The developer controls the Covenants and Restrictions until a specified number of lots have been sold or built upon, thereafter the property owners will be in control and have the potential to make modifications to it, through a Homeowners Association created for the subdivision by the developer.

The importance of Covenants and Restrictions cannot be stressed enough, it protects the developer's substantial financial interest by requiring lot purchasers having their home built by other than the developer, needing the developer's approval of the builder. The house plans will also require the approval of the developer in that they meet all criteria established by the developer for the subdivision.

Homeowners also find protection of their investment through the Covenants and Restrictions from the developer making changes to them, which could negatively affect them financially. The most common potential negative change is by lowering the minimum house square footage requirement to lower construction costs if lot sales have decreased due to a weakening real estate market. Also, by prohibiting certain activities which could affect their property value or enjoyment of the property.

**Covenants and Restrictions protect the developer and buyers by:**

A.) Architectural and Home Construction Standards
B.) Property Use Prohibitions

**Architectural and Home Construction Standards:**

A.) Architectural plan approval of homes not built by the developer
B.) Single family homes
C.) Prohibiting certain architectural styles
D.) Minimum house total square footage (See Note)
E.) Minimum house footprint square footage
F.) Garages required, either attached or separate

G.) Home construction to be completed by a specified date from commencement of construction.)
H.) No clear cutting on lots of trees
I.) Landscaping requirements of lots
J.) Landscaping to be installed within a specified time post house completion
K.) Driveways paved
L.) Pools located at rear of house, no above ground pools

**Property Use Prohibitions**

A.) No commercial uses
B.) No domestic animals excepting dogs and cats, not exceeding the maximum allowed per regulations
C.) No noise, dust, or odor generation
D.) No unregistered vehicles unless garaged
E.) No campers, boats or trailers unless garaged
F.) No outdoor laundry drying
G.) No antennas or satellite dish

# CHAPTER 12

## INFRASTRUCTURE PRE-CONSTRUCTION

### OVERVIEW

This chapter discusses the important necessary steps to undertake prior to commencement of construction of the subdivision infrastructure. These steps are also key to the construction process being performed within its timeline and budget.

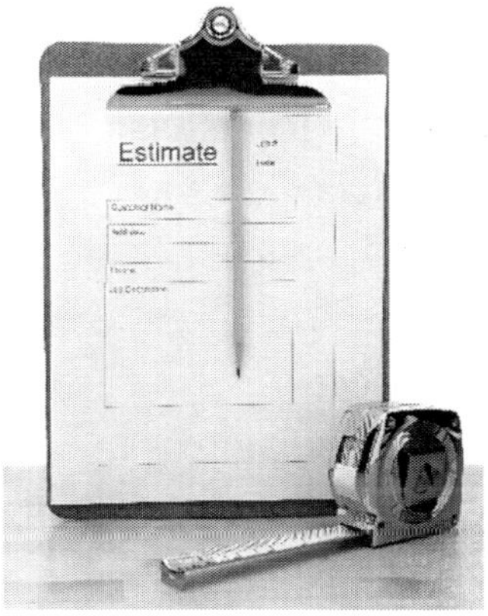


## ESTIMATED INFRASTRUCTUE COSTS

A subdivision's "estimated infrastructure costs" is a crucial tool before issuing a request for contractor bids for installation of infrastructure. Your engineer or construction management/estimator consultant should perform a cost estimate for the infrastructure improvements based upon the approved design plans and other technical information prepared by your engineer for the subdivision. This becomes the base information for comparison between contractor bids.

### LINE ITEMS

Your cost estimate format should be line-item with contractor bids using the identical format, as it provides the best reliability for the developer to analyze them. Lump-sum estimates for major categories of work shall not be accepted as they are difficult to evaluate contractor bid versus contractor bid, and contractor bids versus your engineer's cost estimate.

**Cost Estimate Categories:**

A.) Materials only
B.) Installation only
C.) Combined materials and installation

**Quantity Categories Units:**

A.) Linear feet (LF)
B.) Square feet (SF)
C.) Cubic feet (CF)
D.) Cubic Yard (CY)
E.) Tonnage (Tons)
F.) Acreage (Ac)

## LINE-ITEM ESTIMATE OF INFRASTRUCTURE IMPROVEMENTS

The following infrastructure improvements are typical however, some improvements or services may not be applicable to your subdivision, or there may be a needed improvement or service not included herein, the following should be viewed as an example of what your engineer or construction management consultant would prepare. The following line-items should include any wetlands construction work. The line-item list has been generated based upon major work and service categories.

| CONSTRUCTION SERVICES | QUANTITY | UNITS | $ / UNIT | COST ESTIMATE |
|---|---|---|---|---|
| **Meetings:** | | | | |
| Consultants | | | | |
| Site Contractor | | | | |
| Regulatory Staff & Inspections | | | | |
| **Inspections of Infrastructure Construction**: | | | | |
| Municipality | | | | |
| Developer Engineer/Surveyor | | | | |
| Lenders Agent | | | | |
| **Regulatory Fees**: | | | | |
| Construction Permits | | | | |
| Inspection Fees | | | | |
| Impact Fees | | | | |
| **Road Construction – Initiation:** | | | | |
| Marking Construction Limits of Clearing | | | | |
| Install Construction Fencing | | | | |
| Install Sedimentation Control Devices | | | | |
| Install Vehicle Anti-Tracking Pad(s) | | | | |

| CONSTRUCTION SERVICES | QUANTITY | UNITS | $ / UNIT | COST ESTIMATE |
|---|---|---|---|---|
| **Road Construction – Initial Work:** | | | | |
| Felling of Trees, Clearing Brush | | | | |
| Removal Tree Stumps | | | | |
| Removal Surface Boulders | | | | |
| Rough Grade Road | | | | |
| **Removal Of Existing Manmade Items:** | | | | |
| Abandoned Vehicles | | | | |
| Hazardous Materials | | | | |
| Structures | | | | |
| General Debris | | | | |
| **Remediation/Removal of Contaminated Soil:** | | | | |
| Implement Approved Plan of Remediation | | | | |
| **Layout of Infrastructure Improvements:** | | | | |
| Survey Control – Horizontal & Vertical | | | | |
| Survey Construction Layout | | | | |
| **Excavation of Earth Materials:** | | | | |
| Topsoil – Stockpile for Reuse/Sale | | | | |
| Unsuitable Material Disposal | | | | |
| Suitable Materials Stockpiling | | | | |
| **Ledge Removal:** | | | | |
| Ripping Removal | | | | |
| Blasting Removal | | | | |
| Crushing – For Road, Driveway & Other Uses | | | | |
| Disposal – Burial On-Site or Removal | | | | |
| **Proposed Road Subgrade:** | | | | |
| Fill – Stockpiled Suitable Material | | | | |
| Fill - Imported Material | | | | |
| **Installation Of Sewer/Utility Systems:** | | | | |
| Storm Water Drainage | | | | |
| Road Underdrains | | | | |
| Sewage Main Lines (Public) | | | | |
| Sewage Pump Stations (Public) | | | | |
| Water (Public) | | | | |
| Gas | | | | |

| CONSTRUCTION SERVICES | QUANTITY | UNITS | $ / UNIT | COST ESTIMATE |
|---|---|---|---|---|
| **Storm Water Detention/Retention:** | | | | |
| Excavate Ponding Areas | | | | |
| Subsurface Storage Structures | | | | |
| Riprap Outlet Structures | | | | |
| **Install Road Bedding Materials:** | | | | |
| Gravel | | | | |
| Crushed Stone | | | | |
| **Install Curbs:** | | | | |
| Concrete | | | | |
| Bituminous | | | | |
| **Install Road Pavement (Bituminous):** | | | | |
| Binder Course | | | | |
| Wearing Course | | | | |
| **Utility Trenching – Off Pavement:** | | | | |
| Telephone | | | | |
| Cable | | | | |
| Electric | | | | |
| **Sidewalks:** | | | | |
| Concrete | | | | |
| Bituminous | | | | |
| Rolled Stone | | | | |
| **Guardrails:** | | | | |
| Metal | | | | |
| Timber | | | | |
| **Restoration/Stabilization of Disturbed Areas:** | | | | |
| Geotextile | | | | |
| Loam | | | | |
| Fertilizing | | | | |
| Seeding | | | | |
| Mulching | | | | |
| **Fire Protection:** | | | | |
| Fire Ponds | | | | |
| Fire Water Storage Tanks | | | | |
| Fire Hydrants | | | | |

| CONSTRUCTION SERVICES | QUANTITY | UNITS | $ / UNIT | COST ESTIMATE |
|---|---|---|---|---|
| **Street Lighting:** | | | | |
| Lamp poles | | | | |
| **Signage:** | | | | |
| Traffic Control | | | | |
| Street Signs | | | | |
| Subdivision Entrance Name | | | | |
| **Street Stripping:** | | | | |
| Road Stop Bars | | | | |
| Road Centerlines | | | | |
| Cross Walks | | | | |
| Bike Lanes | | | | |
| **Landscaping:** | | | | |
| Street Trees | | | | |
| Subdivision Entrances | | | | |
| **Miscellaneous** | | | | |
| Porta-Potty | | | | |
| Debris Removal | | | | |
| **As-Built Plans of Infrastructure:** | | | | |
| Survey – Locations & Elevations | | | | |
| Office Survey – As Built Plans | | | | |
| **Unanticipated Services** | | | | |
| **Materials Price Increases** | | | | |
| **Increased Delivery Charges** | | | | |

**ESTIMATED TOTAL COST** $___________

| | QUANTITY | UNITS | $ / UNIT | COST ESTIMATE |
|---|---|---|---|---|

## BID and CONTRACT CRITERIA

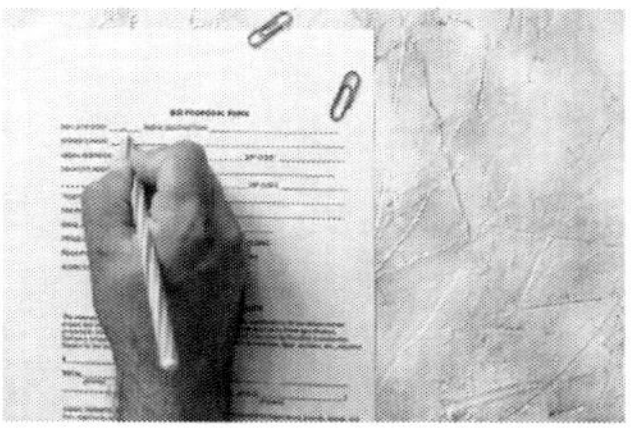

Governmental entities are mandated by law to use public bidding for proposed projects. Any contractor that has an interest in a project may obtain the pertinent bid documents, plans, and submit a bid.

The contractor with the lowest bid tentatively wins the work subject to several reviews. First, that the bid complies with all parameters of the request for bids, and secondly, that the contractor is determined to be qualified to undertake the work. If found not to be in conformance with the bid document criteria or qualified to perform the work, the bid is rejected, and the next lowest bidder is awarded the work subject to the same evaluations.

**Developers being private businesses don't use the public bidding method, they create their own bidding documents and bidder evaluation criteria, and though looking for the most cost-effective bid, are not tied to selecting the lowest bidder.**

Private construction project bidding involves two specific documents. One is a line-item bid request prepared by your engineer or construction management consultant, with bidding instructions prepared by an attorney knowledgeable in construction bidding.

The other document is a contract awarding the work to the successful bidder, which includes the contractor's obligations, time-line schedule of work, payment schedule, penalty clause, a requirement that completed work is acceptable to you the developer, your lender, and the inspectors for the municipality, prior to any payments being made to the contractor.

**Typical Bidding Documents:**

A.) Invitation to Bidders
B.) Description of Project
C.) Bid Specifications
D.) Instructions to Bidders
E.) Bidder References
F.) Bidder Financial Statement
G.) Present and Recent Projects of Bidder
H.) Statement Of Adverse Situations: Bankruptcies; Foreclosures; Judgements; Lawsuit
I.) Non-Collusive Bid Statement
J.) OSHA Form
K.) Project Drawings
L.) Bid Form
M.) Contract Award

**Typical Bidding/Contract Conditions:**

A.) Construction start date and time frame (timeline) for completing specific aspects of work
B.) Contractor compensation schedule (i.e., monthly; percentage of each contract line-item dollar amount for completed work deemed acceptable)

C.) Inspections of work by municipality, developer agent, and if applicable, lenders agent
D.) Correction of work not acceptable to any one of the above inspectors, at contractor expense
E.) Completion deadline exceptions for severe weather conditions or unavailability of materials
F.) Penalties for not meeting specific completion deadlines and unacceptable work
G.) Amount of contract monies to be held after all work is deemed completed, until all infrastructure improvements scheduled to become public property are accepted by the municipality, and any other, non-public work is acceptable to the developer, and the lender
H.) Insurance Coverages: General Liability and Workmen's Compensation (See Note)
I.) Non-Discriminatory Employment Practices
J.) Permitted working hours and non-working days
K.) Equipment refueling spillage reporting and clean-up procedures
L.) Accident and injury reporting procedures

**Contractor Deposit**. Contractors will require a developer to deposit a percentage of the awarded contract for the project either concurrent with the signing of a contract by the parties or prior to commencing work. Two important items must be agreed upon.

The first is who controls the deposit, the contractor, or an attorney for the developer. The second is how and when is the deposit paid to the contractor: as a percentage of each contractor billing; a lump sum at fixed dates or beginning or completing a phase of work; or as the final payment. It could also be another method agreed upon by the parties.

**NOTE:** The selected contractor shall be advised that the responsibility to verify that all subcontractors hired shall have the same insurance coverages per 'H' above.

## FINDING CONTRACTORS

### OVERVIEW

Established developers have a list of contractors that have worked for them or have a good industry reputation. They begin contacting them shortly after submitting a subdivision application, advising them of the anticipated construction start date, and asking if interested in bidding, and if the project schedule fits into theirs.

If you are a first-time subdivision developer you obviously have no contractor list, nor any, or likely much knowledge about specific contractors other than having heard their name. You have work to do in finding suitable contractors to offer them the opportunity to bid on your subdivision. A couple of the best sources to help you locate them are your consultant engineer and attorney.

Your engineer having worked on many subdivisions and other types of construction with various contractors should be able to provide an opinion on those contractors. The principal areas of information you should inquire about: the quality of work; adherence to project schedule; any significant inspection issues and the developer's overall satisfaction with the contractor.

Your attorney may be aware of or can investigate contractors, so you avoid becoming involved with any having a history of disputes with developer's, lawsuits, financial problems, and missing completion deadlines.

**Contractor Red Flags:**

A.) Lis pendens
B.) Judgments
C.) Bankruptcy
D.) Foreclosure
E.) Mechanics liens
F.) Tax liens on construction equipment and/or business property
G.) Suspension of contractor's license
H.) Unfavorable credit history
I.) Frequent change in the business name (may indicate a contractor avoiding financial obligations).

With favorable opinions from your engineer and attorney, you have a list of potential contractors for bidding. But do you have enough contractors? How many is ideal? I would recommend at least six, ideally more. As you become established as a developer you will need fewer contractors for bidding.

As you are new developing subdivisions, you may find some contractors either not responding to your request to bid or submitting very high bids as a way of turning you down while leaving the door open to be considered for a future project. Plentiful work can make this problem worse.

If your contractor list is minimal, you might consider evaluating those who were close to making the cut by gathering any information the municipal engineering/building office has as to the results of their inspections of their work. If the information is favorable, you may have a few more contractors to consider.

As it is the policy of municipalities to not recommend individuals or firms, thereby avoiding favoritism accusations, try the reverse, inquiring about contractors with a frequency of work not passing inspection, now you also have a list of contractors not to contact.

**Appropriate Questions of Your Short List Contractors:**

A.) Location of current and recent subdivision projects
B.) Size of subdivisions; length of roads
C.) Does contractor availability match your anticipated date to start construction
D.) Time to complete work being bid
E.) Any comments, concerns with respect to your subdivision design plans
F.) Years in business, size of staff, long term employees
G.) Equipment, primarily owned or leased
H.) Is contractor self-financed or uses a line of credit
I.) Financial stability of contractor, investigated by your attorney and/or accountant
J.) What new work will you be commencing and when

## EVALUATION OF BIDS

Upon receipt of contractor bids, the next step is analysis of the bids. Only by analysis can an in-depth picture of each bid be understood, it is a key component in selecting a contractor besides the contractor evaluation discussed earlier. Do not make the mistake of focusing as many beginning developer's do, on the lowest dollar amount bid, it can be misleading as to being the best bid, analysis is required.

Analysis of bids can only be accomplished by creating a summary chart of all bids. The analysis should be set up to mirror the line-item categories in your bid document. A summary chart will quickly disclose any significant differences between each contractor in their line-item quotes, both cost and quantities with respect to your engineer's infrastructure line-item estimated costs.

Discuss with your engineer the analysis of the bids, consider any recommendations, but understand you are the one who must make the contractor selection.

By analyzing bids on a line-item basis you can also determine if a bid is front loaded.

**Front Loading**

What is it? It is a bid where the initial stages of construction work are quoted higher than your estimate, while work to be performed later during construction is quoted lower than your estimate. Neither the earlier nor later work quotes will have a favorable comparison to your engineer's estimated infrastructure line-item costs.

I cannot stress enough how much front loading is a very serious problem, it drains your project funds faster than the actual value for work being completed. Even though the total bid amount may be favorable, a front loaded bid significantly increases the risk that in the later stages of work, a contractor who becomes financially stressed and is aware that the remaining contract money is not sufficient to complete work, may request additional money to finish the work, or just abandons your project, as the majority of anticipated profit has already been received due to the front loading of the bid.

## UTILITIES AND UTILITY EASEMENTS

### OVERVIEW

Every subdivision requires utilities to serve the homes to be constructed. Most utilities are provided by private utility companies, while others may be supplied by a municipal, county, or regional agency of government. Two utilities that may be supplied by the developer of the subdivision are a community well for water supply, and a common subsurface sewage disposal system, for a limited number of homes in the subdivision

Ideally, the utilities available for your proposed subdivision are all those necessary for serving it. If some, or all utilities are not at the property, it will require their extension. The questions then are, extension to be by whom and does the developer pay for it?

### UTILITIES

**Utility Extension to Property:**

A.) At developer's expense
B.) Cost sharing, developer, and utility
C.) Without cost to the developer

Construction of the subdivision infrastructure and utility installation generally is not delayed pending extension of a utility to the property. A binding agreement with the utility may need to have been obtained and provided to a municipal regulatory agency.

**Utilities May Be Provided By:**

Municipality
Utility Companies

Regional Authority
Subdivision Developer

**Utilities – Municipal**

| | |
|---|---|
| Water | Installation by municipality or authorized contractor |
| Sewage | Installation by municipality or authorized contractor, or subdivision developer |
| Electric | Installation by municipality or authorized contractor |
| Cable | Installation by municipality or authorized contractor |

**Utilities – Private Companies:**

| | |
|---|---|
| Water | Installation by utility company, or authorized contractor |
| Gas | Installation by utility |
| Electric | Installation by utility |
| Cable | Installation by utility or authorized contractor |
| Phone | Installation by utility |

**Utilities- Regional Authority:**

| | |
|---|---|
| Water | Installation by authority, or authorized contractor |
| Sewer | Installation by municipality, or authorized contractor, or subdivision developer |

**Utilities – Developer:**

| | |
|---|---|
| Water | Installation by developers' contractor |
| | Owner initially or permanent the developer |
| | Paid by developer |
| | Homeowners Association, successor to developer? |

**NOTE:** Certain utility providers may permit the contractor for the subdivision developer to participate in aspects of the installation of the utility such as: clearing of installation area; providing trenching; providing bedding material and/or its placement in trench; filing of trench; and restoration of disturbed area.

## UTILITY EASEMENTS

Every utility will specify the type of easement they require within the subdivision prior to entering into an agreement to install their service. In Connecticut, the principal utility easement of a subdivision encompassed the right-of-way width and length of all its roads, with a deed description of the easement being coincidental with the road geometry of the filed subdivision map. All utilities could be installed within this easement.

If the subdivision contains private roads or shared private common driveways serving multiple lots, the utility easement width is specified by the power company, it was of sufficient width that telephone and cable services were able to be accommodated within the easement. The power company required a deeded easement with its description based upon an easement map prepared by the developer's land surveyor which will be filed in the municipal land records. Telephone and cable utilities generally only require a deeded grant of easement, no separate easement map.

**CAUTION.** If a developer wants to modify the location of a road, private road, or shared common driveway burdened with a utility easement, a new easement will be required for the utilities.

However, the original utility easement(s) will remain, as the general practice of utility companies is to use easements acquired as collateral for their borrowing. The utilities have also bundled your easement(s) with easements from other subdivisions, unwinding your original easement from a collateral bundle of different subdivision easements will be resisted or refused, so you will still have the original easements which would exclude their area from physical use, such as for construction of a structure.

## OFF SITE IMPROVEMENTS

### OVERVIEW

Offsite improvements for a proposed subdivision are often required when the proposed subdivision road(s) access is by connection to an existing public road.

Whether the public road is local, county or State, concerns about the proposed connection are generally similar. They were discussed in, "Chapter 6 – Buyer Due Diligence: Post Signed Contract, Part One – Always Investigate: Accessing A Subdivision from a State Highway", the focus then being on obtaining the best assurance possible that a subdivision road connection was likely, before final commitment to continue on towards eventually submitting an application for action to subdivide.

#### Design Plans – Typical Concerns:

A.) **Adequate Sightline** – Exiting traffic from the subdivision road at its junction with the existing road and traffic on the existing road must both be able to see each other. The extent of sightline improvement is based upon the stopping distance for the posted speed limit.

B.) **Safe Access and Egress** – Traffic on the existing road (especially State highways) may pose a safety risk to vehicles attempting to access or exit from the subdivision road for vehicles on either road, necessitating installation of a bypass lane, or deceleration lane, or both, or a traffic signal.

C.) **Subdivision Storm Water Road Drainage** – For a subdivision road which drains towards existing road, it must be determined if the subdivision has a right to introduce its drainage into the existing road drainage system, if not, designing a retention system within the subdivision.

The process with the respective highway entity after a site inspection with their staff and your engineer, will be the preparation of a plan, a drainage analysis, and to demonstrate that the sightline stopping distance required is obtainable.

Upon obtaining approval of the subdivision plan by the municipal regulatory agency, submit the approval to the state highway for their approval and issuance of a permit to make the required modifications upon the highway right-of-way. Upon approval by the highway entity, request a site meeting before commencement of work to discuss safety procedures, maintenance of traffic flow, and if coordination needs to be arranged with any utility providers whose facilities may be affected by the work.

# CHAPTER 13

## LOT ASKING PRICES

### OVERVIEW

Long before the end of most subdivision infrastructure construction, it is time to focus on determining the asking prices for lots and how many lots will initially be offered for sale.

## DETERMINATION OF BASE COST OF LOTS

**First step.** Determine which of the three real estate markets described below, is your market situation, as the rate of lot absorption of each is different, a consideration in setting asking prices.

**Real estate market situations (typical):**

A.) Strong market demand, buyers paying asking price, and ability to increase prices as sales progress

B.) Normal market demand, sales at a steady rate, some negotiating of asking price with buyers, price increases less robust and less frequent

C.) Slow market demand, negotiating with buyers on asking price, no price increases

**Second step.** Determine the total project expenses. Some expenses below may not apply to your project.

**Expenses 'A'** These are both known expenses, plus estimated expenses of remaining work per the line items of the awarded bid

**A.) Development Expenses – Fixed:**

1.) Purchase price of land and associated closing costs

2.) Infrastructure construction costs including utilities and off-site improvements, if any

3.) Consultant fees including legal
4.) Municipal application and inspection fees
5.) Financing costs for land purchase and/or infrastructure construction
6.) Performance bond financing cost
7.) Liability insurance
8.) Any other expenditures
9.) Maintenance bond financing

**Expenses 'B'** These are variable expenses and may have an unknown length of time before terminating

**B.) Development Expenses – Projected:**

1.) Maintenance of property, post construction
2.) Property taxes
3.) Realtor sales commissions
4.) Lot sales closing costs and legal
5.) Unanticipated expenses

**Third Step.** Preliminary base cost of lots.

**Expenses A + Expenses B ÷ Number of Lots = Base Cost of Lots**

**Fourth Step.** Effect upon the Base Cost of Lots, consider these potential decreases of expenses over time.

**Development Expenses – Potential Decreases:**

A.) Property taxes and liability insurance decrease as lots are sold
B.) Maintenance bonds typically expire not later than two years after acceptance of improvements by the municipality, this expense may terminate before all lots are sold
C.) Maintenance of common subdivision property will become the responsibility of a homeowner's association once a designated number of lots have been sold
D.) Financing payments, if any, will likely end before all lots have been sold

**Final Step.** Adjusted base cost of lots.

**Adjusted Base Cost of Lots = Base Cost of Lots – Potential Development Expenses Decrease**

# DETERMINING LOT ASKING PRICES

## Lot Valuation Adjustments

Individual lot values can vary because of the physical effect of one or more factors, such as, terrain, ledge outcrops, wetlands, zoning buildable area, and the aesthetics of a lot.

When this is the case, a lot having one or more of the above factors would require them to be applied to the adjusted base cost of lots to arrive at the base value of that lot.

The amount of any adjustment applied is a judgment call of the developer, for a new developer I recommend having an appraiser or realtor to advise you.

Established developers generally make a seat-of-the-pants decision from a walk-through of the subdivision as they draw upon their prior subdivision experiences in making this adjustment.

## Base Lot Asking Price

Upon completing the lot valuation adjustments and arriving at the base value of a lot, you are now able to establish its base asking price by adding to it, the profit you seek.

## Listed Lot Asking Prices

The last step is to then determine what the listed asking price of a lot will be. You may use the base asking price, but I recommend increasing it by a factor to compensate for prospective buyers making offers lower than the listing price, this will preserve some or all of your desired profit.

**Once the lot asking prices are set, consider the following**:

A.) Listing for sale only a portion of the lots, a mixture of lots of differing quality and prices

B.) List lots only where road access is sufficiently completed to allow passenger vehicle access

C.) Lot asking prices are generally able to be increased over time as the subdivision is being built, reserve an adequate number of the best lots for the end, they will help to maximize profits.

Lot listing prices should be evaluated at appropriate times during the life of marketing the subdivision, this provides information to determine whether prices should be held, or that increases are justified.

# CHAPTER 14

## INFRASTRUCTURE CONSTRUCTION

### OVERVIEW

This chapter discusses the necessary steps to be commenced after completing "Chapter Twelve Pre-Construction Infrastructure." You will cover topics such as: the start-up of construction; specific actions necessary during construction; inspections during construction; contractor payments; and keeping to your project Timeline and budget.

## PERFORMANCE BONDS

Performance bonds serve the purpose of protecting both the municipality where the subdivision is located, and any purchasers of lots or homes, while the subdivision infrastructure is still being installed.

The bond's purpose is to provide the funds for the completion of the work to install the subdivision infrastructure for a failed subdivision. The calling of a performance bond Is restricted only to a subdivision with partially completed infrastructure, and when there are homes, or lots owned by third parties other than the developer.

**Infrastructure includes, but is not limited to:** a

A.) Roads including its storm drainage
B.) Fire protection
C.) Post development water management structures
D.) Utilities, whether private, public or subdivision association
E.) Offsite improvements

The amount of the performance bond is generally based upon a conservative estimate by the engineer of the municipality. The amount of the bond will also likely include a safety cushion for inflation on the assumption that if called, likely several years will have passed since the bond amount was set. So, keep in mind that you should anticipate the bond amount to be higher than your engineer's estimate or the bid amount of the winning contractor.

The performance bond may also include maintenance costs for snow plowing and road sanding or deicing and mowing of grass along the road shoulders.

**NOTE:** Subdivisions having proposed infrastructure improvements where commencement of construction has not begun, or where it has commenced but no homes or lots have been conveyed to a third party, excepting on a completed road or an existing public road, it would not be the responsibility of the municipality to call the performance bond and either commence or complete the installation of remaining infrastructure.

Possible situations that may occasionally arise when the infrastructure is uncompleted, and where there are homes and/or lots owned by third parties, presents a challenge as to whom is responsible to resume installation of remaining infrastructure, and whether an entity other than the municipality may access the performance bond.

**Situations, such as:**

A.) Foreclosure of developer by a lender
B.) Developer filing bankruptcy
C.) Planning and Zoning Commission declaring the subdivision **"null and void"** for failure to complete the infrastructure improvements within the statutory time for completion

In Chapter Eleven the three types of bonding were discussed: cash; surety bond; and lender letter of credit. If the bond is a cash bond jointly in the names of the municipality and developer, and the bonding agreement has a clause permitting upon a developer default the immediate access to the funds by the municipality, completion of the infrastructure can quickly be resumed at least from the perspective of having the funds available.

However, a surety bond or letter of credit, especially the later, may require negotiation between the bond issuer and the municipality as to when availability of funds can be expected, whether funds will be lump sum or by installments, and possibly other factors. These latter two bonding methods will lengthen how soon work can commence and how long it could take to be completed.

# COMMENCEMENT AND COMPLETION DEADLINES

## OVERVIEW

If you are new to developing subdivision's you will typically find in addition to the deadlines to record an approved subdivision in the land records, as discussed in Chapter 11, commencement and completion dates imposed by a regulatory agency.

### Planning & Zoning Commission

Commencement of subdivision infrastructure installation is not normally an issue with developers however, there is no guarantee that certain conditions of approval could be unfavorable, such as:

A.) Substantial completion of construction in a section or area of the subdivision before beginning any construction activities elsewhere in the subdivision.

B.) Utilities requiring extension to the subdivision shall be installed by the providers to the subdivision before utility installation can begin within the subdivision.

C.) Seasonal start and or stop dates for construction

The Planning and Zoning Commission notifies applicants upon approval of their subdivision of the state statute deadline date for completion of all infrastructure. Connecticut statutes require that infrastructure be completed within five years of approval of the subdivision.

At the request of the developer if infrastructure is not fully completed and prior to reaching said date, the commission may extend the deadline date. As there is always a risk that a commission would not grant an extension, a prudent developer's goal is to be finished with construction well before said date. Extensions are looked upon favorably for situations outside of developer control such as, extremely brutal winter weather, regional or national shortages of key construction materials, natural disasters, and other similar severe situations.

Appeal of the approval of a subdivision by an aggrieved party to Superior Court postpones the commencement of the five-year construction period until the appeal is concluded.

Another tool developer's use on large subdivisions to reduce the risk of not meeting the five-year deadline or obtaining an extension is to develop the subdivision in two or more sections, with the size of a section matched to a comfortable time frame to complete its infrastructure construction.

### Inland Wetlands Commission

The Inland Wetlands Commission in addition to its deadline date for completion of all work per their approved regulated activity permit, might impose other conditions which could cause time delays for non-wetlands construction, generally the bulk of construction.

A.) Seasonal start and or stop dates for construction

B.) Specific sequence of commencement of work when there are multiple permitted areas.

C.) Completion of all work at a permit area before being able to begin work on another permitted site.

## ENVIRONMENTAL PROTECTION INSTALLATIONS

### OVERVIEW

Environmental protection is a focus of both the Planning and Zoning and Inland Wetlands Commissions. Subdivisions approved by both commissions will include different types of protections for inland wetlands and uplands.

### Planning & Zoning Commission

The Planning and Zoning Commission focus is to keep disturbed soil due to excavation and filling activities during construction of the infrastructure of the subdivision from exiting the construction area and negatively impacting undisturbed uplands and wetlands.

To contain erosion of exposed soils during construction, the following describes the typical actions taken. Land is classed as primarily either woodland or non-woodland. As Connecticut has a high percentage of woodland I'll begin with it, if you are in non-woodland area just by-pass my beginning description.

Silt fencing is Installed at the limit of construction either as the initial activity or prior to the felling of trees, depending on access and terrain issues. After useful tree trunks are removed, stump and brush removal with heavy equipment begins. Topsoil for both woodland and non-woodland sites is next removed and stockpiled with a silt fence surround, then excavation of unsuitable soils and removal of surface boulders follows.

Placement of fill materials and or excavation of suitable soil continues until the road subgrade is finished, followed by lifts of subbase material and gravel subbase compacted per standards and then the binder course of bituminous pavement.

Generally, the greatest area disturbed in subdivisions is for construction of roads. The next greatest areas disturbed are for the creation of post construction storm water runoff management detention and retention ponding areas.

**Inland Wetland Commission**

The Inland Wetland Commission has jurisdiction over uplands beyond the inland wetland boundary for the distance specified in their regulations. The commission is focused on protections both during and post construction within inland wetlands and the regulated upland area.

**During construction – temporary protection:**

A.) Silt fencing, staked in place

B.) Hay bales, staked in place, commonly used in wetlands or swales subject to intermittent water flow

C.) Geo-textile catch basin inserts, prior to paving of roads and until adjoining soil is stabilized

D.) Hay coverage of disturbed slopes

**Disturbed areas – permanent protection:**

A.) Flat areas to moderate slopes: topsoil, seed, fertilizing and mulch

B.) Steep slopes: as above but using bio-degradable fabric for stability

C.) Rip rap at storm water point discharge outlets

D.) Sheet water swales at storm water point discharge outlets

Temporary protection devices must be maintained during construction, especially after heavy rainfall which requires early inspection to detect and repair any breaches. Protective devices must remain in place until inspectors deem the disturbed areas to be permanently stabilized.

Post construction protection consists of permanent installations, both constructed and natural, with natural protections being monitored until stabilization is complete.

Some protections required by the Planning and Zoning and Wetland Commissions may duplicate each other when the protection area of each commission overlaps the other. In that instance portions of bonding can be duplicative.

# CONSTRUCTION DEBRIS DISPOSAL

## OVERVIEW

Construction of a subdivision's infrastructure and homes, creates substantial amounts of both natural and man-made waste. Where can it be disposed of, by what method, what equipment is required, and are there specific disposal regulations in place?

The subdivision regulations of the Connecticut municipalities where my consultant practice was focused, all had regulations specific for disposal of unsuitable materials. Additionally, Connecticut statewide had banned the burning of all combustible materials.

Disposal regulations were adopted to end the prior practices of most builders of burying virtually everything, and wherever in a subdivision. This practice often resulted in problems years later for homeowners. See, "Chapter Six, Part Two, What's Buried? What Can Be Buried?," for more discussion.

### Typical Concerns / Regulations

**Concerns With Burial:**

A.) Leachate from trees and stumps contaminating groundwater, wetlands, and watercourses

B.) Decomposition of burial debris causing land settlement

C.) Homeowners needing to excavate and remove buried debris before being able to build an addition to the house, or to install an inground swimming pool.

**Regulations to Bury/Dispose – Infrastructure and Home Construction Debris:**

A.) Trees – portions not harvested for timber or firewood, chipped, used onsite for landscaping

B.) Brush and undergrowth – chipped, incorporated with tree chips

C.) Stumps – ground up either on or offsite, disposal generally required offsite

D.) Boulders and blasted ledge – burial on lots in area prohibited for construction (between property lines and building setback lines) or crushed onsite to use as subbase material for roads, driveways, etc.

E.) Bituminous pavement and curbing – disposal offsite

F.) Non-wood, non-toxic materials – burial between property lines and building setback lines

G.) Wood – removal offsite

H.) Toxic materials – removal offsite

## INSPECTIONS OF INFRASTRUCTURE INSTALLATIONS

Infrastructure offered to a municipality will be inspected by:

A.) The municipal agency staff, typically the town engineer, or

B.) A municipal consultant construction management firm, or

C.) A municipal consultant professional engineer

The purpose of these mandated inspections during construction are to minimize post municipal acceptance, the potential need for public monies for corrective work due to the failure of inferior construction.

However, a prudent developer should not rely on inspections by agents of the municipality. Why? It is based upon Risk Management, a key component of your protection.

For protection of your significant investment to install the subdivision infrastructure, and assurance that upon its completion it will be accepted by the municipality relieving you of financial responsibility, i.e., risk.

You can best minimize your risk by having the infrastructure inspected during construction by your engineer or a construction management consultant. The concurrence of your inspector with the municipal inspector is the best assurance that the subdivision infrastructure will be accepted by the municipality, ending your risk.

Additionally, if financing is involved for the subdivision, the lender will have their construction inspector determine upon each request for additional funds to pay the contractor, that the completed work conforms to the design plans and meets accepted standards of construction, another reduction of your risk.

## CONTRACTOR PAYMENTS

Typical funding sources for contractor payments:

A.) Developer cash funds

B.) Lender financed funds

C.) Combination of 'A and B'

D.) Partial release(s) of a cash performance bond by the Planning and Zoning Commission

During the construction period payments will be made from one or more of the above sources. For subdivisions with a lengthy time frame for infrastructure construction, contractor billing should be based upon the percentage of work completed per line-items, as described in the awarded line-item bid.

Typically, billing is monthly, alternatively instead of monthly it could be based upon completion of work in a specific line-item or group of line-items. In any case, anticipate many partial bills while construction is ongoing. Payment of billing as above cited, shall be tied to satisfactory inspection of said construction cited in the contractor bill and concurrently the delivery to the developer of a contractor lien waiver for said work.

## OFF-SITE IMPROVEMENTS

### OVERVIEW

Off-site improvements can be a condition of approval of the Planning and Zoning Commission for a subdivision. The off-site improvements may be on a municipal road or a state highway. Improvements necessary for a municipal road will be part of the subdivision application process. For any improvements on a state highway, a separate permit process with the state will be necessary.

**Typical off-site improvements:**

A.) Subdivision storm water drainage connecting to a state drainage system, would be subject to an existing right to do so, or the granting of the right by the state, and installing required improvements.
B.) Sight line improvements within the road or highway right-of-way
C.) Widening of the existing travelled way of a road or state highway
D.) Addition of a by-pass or deceleration lane, or both, to the existing road or highway
E.) Signalization at the intersection of the subdivision road with the state highway

Successful completion of off-site road/highway improvements may be a prerequisite for either obtaining a municipal building permit to construct a home, or a certificate of occupancy for a home.

# CHAPTER 15

## INFRASTRUCTURE POST CONSTRUCTION

### OVERVIEW

This chapter covers the several areas of post infrastructure construction including the activities the developer will need to complete to conclude the development phase of the subdivision, independent of any building activities on subdivision lots.

## AS – BUILT PLANS OF INFRASTRUCTURE IMPROVEMENTS

Most subdivisions have one or more proposed roads for access, excepting subdivisions of small size and/or with extensive frontage on existing roads.

Proposed subdivision roads are almost always intended to eventually become public roads owned and maintained by the municipality. To protect itself from accepting inferior constructed infrastructure in addition to its inspections during installation of improvements, it requires as-built plans demonstrating that the improvements agree with the approved subdivision plans. The following list of improvements for a subdivision (not all may apply) are provided to give the reader a better understanding of the numerous components typically involved.

**Installation of roads and associated infrastructure, such as, but not limited to:**

- A.) Removal of topsoil and stockpiling for reuse
- B.) Removal of any unsuitable soils
- C.) Excavation of suitable subbase soils to, and or placement of subbase materials to, proposed subgrade
- D.) Storm water road drainage system
- E.) Utilities – under proposed road pavement
- F.) Installation of aggregate base material to proposed grade
- G.) Pavement – binder course

H.) Curb installation – bituminous (if concrete or granite, prior to binder course)
I.) Pavement – wearing surface (top course)
J.) Sidewalks
K.) Storm water drainage – detention/retention structures
L.) Utilities – off pavement
M.) Stabilization of disturbed areas
N.) All other improvements per the approved design plans

The documentation of a subdivisions installed improvements follows the steps outlined next.

**First Step – Verification and Location**
Determining the location, grades, and elevations of installed improvements by field survey, visual inspection of structures, and appropriate measurements of improvements, all to determine if they agree within accepted tolerances with the various design plans.

**Second Step – Office Compilation**

The locations, measurements, and other collected site information are calculated and combined into a base working drawing which allows for comparison with the design plan to determine if installed infrastructure is in conformance within the accepted tolerances.

The following are a more detailed description.

A.) Road – Verify pavement (traveled way) meets its design location within the road right-of-way (street lines), meets its specified width, and curbs meet the specified height per the Road Construction Plan.
B.) That the road, its storm water drainage system, and its public sewer system (if any), including the following: catch basins; manholes; pipe types; pipe sizes; and pipe inverts, conform to the locations, grades, and elevations depicted on the Road Construction Plan
C.) The following improvements (if proposed): sidewalks, street lighting, street trees, street signs, and landscaping meet the location and elevations depicted on the Site Development Plan and/or Road Construction Plan.
D.) Utility poles and utility vaults (surface) for underground utilities, control valves for potable water supply and public gas, fire protection such as, hydrants, fire ponds, or fire water storage tanks, and any other improvements conform to the locations depicted on the afore mentioned plans

**Final Step – "As-Built-Plans"**

These plans are the permanent documentation that the installed improvements concur within accepted tolerances to the approved design plans, permitting the municipality to act on accepting said improvements by the municipality and ending the developer's responsibilities.

## MONUMENTATION OF ROADS AND LOTS

### OVERVIEW

Subdivision regulations will most likely require that permanent monumentation be set upon all road right-of-way lines, also known as street lines, for all roads proposed to be accepted by the municipality as a public road.

Monumentation is extremely important to establish the precise location of a road right-of-way as it is coincidental with the front property line of lots on said roads. Monumentation may also be required to be set at other locations in the subdivision.

Monumentation of the street line is key as it allows for surveyors in the future other than the original surveyor of the subdivision, to be able to survey individual properties and set any desired monumentation.

**Monumentation locations typically required:**

A.) Front lot corners, only
B.) Diagonal lot corners, only
C.) All lot corners
D.) All lot corners and property line angle points
E.) Access way to rear lots (a.k.a. interior or flag lots)

**Monumentation that may be required:**

A.) Open space
B.) Fire protection facility easements
C.) Shared driveways serving multiple lots
D.) Drainage easements upon lots
E.) Road sight line easements upon lots
F.) Utility or sewer easements upon lots
G.) Other areas or facilities within the subdivision

The type of permanent monumentation required to be set may be specified in the subdivision regulations or left to the determination of the subdivision land surveyor, based upon the soil conditions encountered at each location.

**Typical types of monumentation:**

A.) Concrete, pre-cast, 36" length
B.) Cut stone, such as, granite, 36" length (uncommon today as expensive)
C.) Iron rod, such as, re-bar, 30" or 36" length
D.) Brass disk, center point field punched or pre-cast cross, used in ledge and existing concrete and stone structures
E.) Drill hole, set in exposed ledge and existing concrete or stone structures
F.) Concrete field poured where ledge is deeper than 'D' or 'E' above, brass disk or drill hole set post hardening
G.) Iron rod or pipe set in marsh or swampy soils, length can be in excess of 5' (feet).

Although not part of the monumentation occurring as one of the last items in completing the subdivision, some municipalities require certain monumentation to be installed before the following:

A.) Offering lots for sale
B.) Obtaining individual home building permits
C.) Obtaining a certificate of occupancy for a home

## ACCEPTAMCE OF INFRASTRUCTURE IMPROVEMENTS

### SUBDIVISION IMPROVEMENTS

The acceptance process for a municipality to assume permanent responsibility for specific subdivision infrastructure improvements, such as, roads, storm water drainage systems, public sewer system, and fire protection facilities, involves numerous steps to minimize the financial risk to the municipality in assuming ownership of said improvements.

The initial step entailed numerous inspections during installation of said improvements by the municipalities staff or its agents. This was followed by as-built plans of said completed infrastructure improvements.

Where required, the last step is monumentation of the subdivision road right-of-way(s), lot property lines, and other facilities not the responsibility of either individual lot owners or the subdivision association.

As part of the acceptance process, any off-site subdivision improvements, release of the performance bond, submitting of a maintenance bond if required, will need to be finalized to the satisfaction of the commission.

When the above are deemed satisfactory by the Planning and Zoning Commission, it can vote to approve the developer's request for the acceptance of the infrastructure improvements as public property. A favorable vote is the commission's recommendation to the municipalities governing body i.e., Board of Selectmen, Town Manager, Mayor, etc. the body with the authority to accept improvements and assume responsibility.

### OFF-SITE IMPROVEMENTS

Earlier we discussed off-site improvements necessary for obtaining approval of the subdivision, see "Chapter 12 – Infrastructure Pre-Construction" and "Chapter 14 – Infrastructure Construction".

Off-site improvements may have taken place on either an existing municipal road or state highway. In the instance of a municipal road, the acceptance of both the off-site improvements and internal subdivision road and improvements would likely be a concurrent action of the Planning and Zoning Commission. Depending upon the significance of the off-site improvement(s), if relatively minor, inspection by municipal staff or agents may be adequate to recommend acceptance. If the improvements are substantial, an as-built plan may be required as with internal subdivision road improvements.

If the off-site improvements are on a state highway, their acceptance upon completion by the state must be obtained before the municipality will accept the subdivision road(s) connecting to the state highway.

## PERFORMANCE BOND RELEASE

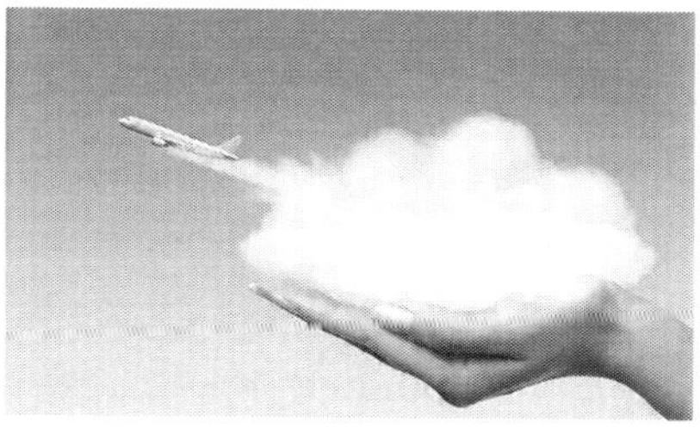

The performance bond for subdivision infrastructure improvements likely has been substantially reduced from its initial amount due to a series of approvals of partial bond releases by the Planning and Zoning Commission.

Developer's typically request partial bond reductions as portions of the subdivision infrastructure have been completed and also determined by the municipality to be satisfactory upon inspection.

The remainder of the performance bond will be released to the developer upon acknowledgement by the Planning and Zoning Commission that all subdivision infrastructure improvements are completed and meet all standards.

However, depending upon the regulations of the municipality, the remainder of the performance bond may be applied towards, or in lieu of, posting a separate maintenance bond.

## MAINTENANCE BOND POSTING AND RELEASE

### BOND POSTING

When the Planning and Zoning Commission is considering a developer's request to accept all subdivision infrastructure improvements by the municipality, the commission is aware that upon authorizing acceptance that the municipality assumes perpetual responsibility to maintain, repair or replace all said improvements.

The greatest potential future financial exposure is generally with roads. To guard against the premature failure of improvements and the financial implications for the municipality, a maintenance bond is required from the developer. It shall become effective concurrently with acceptance of the infrastructure improvements by the municipality and release of the performance bond.

A typical maintenance bond term is two years, the amount of the bond determined by regulations or the specific financial concern as to a subdivision's infrastructure improvements. The type of maintenance bond likely will be the same as the performance bond, either a cash bond, a letter of credit, or a surety bond.

### BOND RELEASE

Prior to the expiration date of the maintenance bond, the municipality will have all infrastructure improvements inspected to determine that maintenance, repair, or replacement is not required.

If the condition of the infrastructure is found to be satisfactory, the Planning and Zoning Commission will release the maintenance bond to the developer, ending any further responsibility of the developer for the infrastructure of the subdivision.

# CHAPTER 16

## IMPORTANT CONSIDERATIONS

### OVERVIEW

This chapter covers topics which are not as interrelated as most content is, in the other chapters, however these topics are especially important for a successful subdivision project, whether only once, but especially if you want to create a subdivision development business.

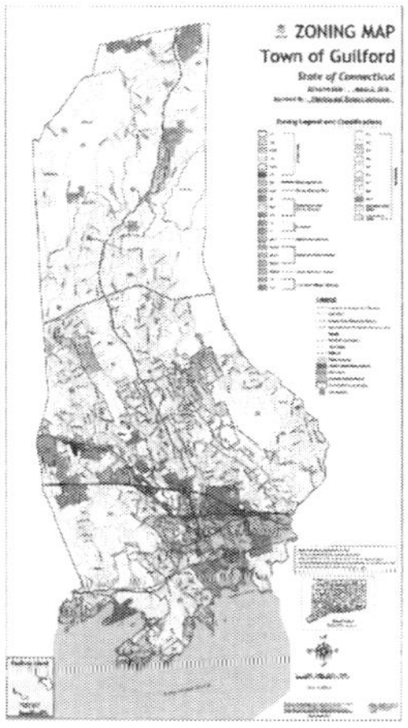


## ZONE CHANGE

A zone change is always problematic and needs to be evaluated very carefully before attempting it.

In my professional practice it was quite uncommon to find a residentially zoned property having other than a single zone. Commercial or industrial properties were more frequent in having two zones, such as, two different commercial or industrial zones or a combination of a commercial and an industrial zone.

Let me get straight to my recommendation, until you have experience from having completed multiple development projects, I say you should stay away from a property with other than a single zone.

**Zoning – Problematic Property:**

A.) Property in two different residential zones
B.) Proposing to down zone a single zone residential property
C.) An undeveloped, residentially zoned property surrounded by commercial or industrial zoned property.

**Should any be considered for your subdivision?**
Be aware that in pursuing a proposed change in a property's zoning, your timeline will need to be extended, postponing when you are able to begin design of a subdivision, let

alone submission of its application for subdivision. This goes against the perennial goal of obtaining approval as quickly as possible and getting to market with your project.

Zone change applications can generate serious opposition, proceed only if necessary for the project. If a zone change application is successful, those opposed to the change may very well now focus their opposition on your application for subdivision when it comes before the Planning and Zoning Commission. Not a welcome situation.

**First Situation – Property located in two or more residential zones.**

The most significant difference between zones will be the lot standards, particularly area and street frontage requirements. Attempting to change the portion of the property zoned with more restrictive standards to the zone with lower (more favorable) standards, thereby increasing the lot yield of the entire proposed subdivision, will likely be frowned upon by the commission. I do not recommend trying it, it is "tilting at windmills."

A possible work-around would be to combine the zone change subject to developing the property as an Open Space Development Subdivision, creating significantly more open space than a standard development of the property per its existing zones. See, "Chapter 8 – Subdivision Design, Open Space Development Subdivisions". As this method of subdivision development is structured to minimize the area to be built upon, reduce infrastructure, and from the public perspective, leave a very substantial percentage of the property undisturbed as open space, it potentially is the key to moderating or eliminating opposition and obtaining approval.

**Second Situation – Down zoning of a single zone property:**

Down zoning proposes to rezone a property from its present zone to a zone with less restrictive standards. The principal outcome would be smaller lots, resulting in more lots. This is unlikely to be of interest to a Zoning Commission. Is there a way to interest the commission in doing so? Possibly, if the commission can see a definite benefit to the municipality.

Possible benefit #1. As mentioned in the First Situation above, an Open Space Development Subdivision with its significant open space may be of interest to the commission.

Possible benefit #2. A portion of the subdivision be dedicated to affordable housing. This however would probably only be of interest if you are also building the homes, or you have a homebuilder partner.

Possible benefit #3. If there is a need for accessory apartments for the aging parents of the residents of the municipality. My professional experience in my Connecticut consultant practice was that an accessory apartment was only permitted for an existing house.

If the zoning commission was receptive to allowing accessory apartments with new home construction, it might be approvable.

**Third Situation – Undeveloped residential property surrounded by non-residential property:**

A.) This is a property to avoid as a potential residential subdivision unless the property is massive in area, effectively creating its own world, irrespective of the surrounding non-residential property.

B.) If the non-residentially zoned properties are significantly vacant of improvements, there may be a possibility for developing the residential subdivision. The Zoning Commission may have perceived a future need for this type of commercial development in this area, but the market has obviously said otherwise. So, if years or decades have passed with only minimal development, the owners of said zoned properties may be receptive to changing the zoning to residential. If successful, then the existing residentially zoned property would then become a viable candidate to develop.

**Remember:** Zone change must be evaluated as to the likelihood of success, as it postpones the ability to begin design of the subdivision and increases the timeline for the project. Also, any opposition the proposed zone change may have stirred up, could result in the opposition then focusing on your subdivision .

## PRIVATE ROADS

Private roads when permitted for subdivisions must be carefully evaluated as to whether they will be beneficial beyond implying that a subdivision is "exclusive."

My area of professional practice in Connecticut had very few municipalities with regulations permitting private roads. The discussion herein is specific to the positives and negatives for the developer considering a private road subdivision.

Even though I was involved in only one proposed private road subdivision, my expectations as to a concern about the value of a private road subdivision for my client was substantiated the further the design phase progressed.

The property was located in the Town of Killingworth, a town with significant vacant land both as it was slightly beyond the range of active subdivision development in adjoining towns but also because of the vast land tracts owned by three entities, an exclusive private hunting and fishing club, the reservoirs and watersheds of two private water companies, and several Connecticut State Forest land tracts and one State Park.

My client who had inherited several large woodland properties throughout the town, decided that unlike the others that I had designed as standard subdivisions, that a property which contained quite a large wetland be designed as a subdivision served by a private road.

**Positives Private Road:**

Private roads cost significantly less to construct as they were not required to be paved nor have stormwater drainage systems, relying upon sheet flow off the edge of the road into either drainage swales running parallel to the road or further into the adjoining land . This is an immediate benefit to the developer.

A private road represented to prospective purchasers as having a privacy benefit and exclusivity, had a fly in the ointment which they may have missed, regulations prohibited gating of the road entrance.

**Private Road Negatives – Developer:**

A.) Permanent cul-de-sac roads had a maximum length significantly shorter than a public road

B.) Minimum lot area and lot road frontage were greater than for public roads, decreasing lot yield

C.) Developer must create and initially fund an account for the future replacement of the road

D.) Developer must establish an annual road maintenance budget, including snow plowing, and fund it for the first year

E.) The developer had to create a homeowner's association and grant it the fee to the road

**Private Road Negatives – Purchasers:**

A.) School buses were prohibited from serving private roads, necessitating constructing a bus stop shelter for protection of children from winter weather at the private road entrance.

B.) The only municipal services vehicles permitted to access a private road were emergency services

C.) As private roads are not public property, they are assessed and taxed like other private property

D.) The homeowner's association was responsible for collecting and paying the annual property tax

E.) No decrease in property assessments were considered due to the decrease in public services

As you can see there were significantly more negatives than positives with private roads, give them careful consideration before committing to their use in a project of yours unless the regulations are significantly more favorable for the developer and purchasers.

## START OF HOME CONSTRUCTION

Assuming that you are planning on not being the builder of the homes in your subdivision but solely the developer, you will have two types of lot buyers, established home builders who will buy one or more lots for speculative and/or contract building, and individuals desiring to have a custom home built by a builder of their choice.

For the first, you need to determine that you are selling lots to a quality homebuilder, for the second, you need to have evaluation standards in place for approving/disapproving a potential homebuilder for that type of buyer.

For both, there are four key standards that you must inform them of prior to making an offer to purchase:

A.) Your approval of house plans

B.) That development of their lot is in conformance with the Declaration of Covenants and Restrictions

C.) Construction will be monitored as to being in conformance with the approved plans

D.) There is a time frame for completion of construction from commencement

**Warning.** Avoid allowing an individual purchaser of a lot to function as the home builder or general contractor. It is potentially nothing but problems for you in enforcing the standards specified in your Declaration of Covenants and Restrictions.

**Criteria to Start Construction (typical):**

**What regulation requirements must you meet prior to:**

A.) Offering lots for sale

B.) Selling a lot

C.) Purchasers obtaining a building permit for a house

**Degree of infrastructure improvements required:**

A.) Road sub-base installed
B.) Road binder pavement installed
C.) Fire protection installed

**Home building permit issuance may be dependent upon:**

A.) Potable water supply available
B.) Electric service available
C.) Fire protection functionable

**Sequential building permit method (if policy):**

A.) Blasting permit (if required)
B.) On-site well installed (if applicable)
C.) Footing/foundation permit
D.) House permit (with all sub permits, and A, B & C completed/installed/approved)

For lots served by individual on-site subsurface sewage disposal systems, approval of a system design plan and issuance of a permit, will be required prior to issuing one or more of the above permits.

## FRONTING AND DISCOUNTING LOTS TO HOMEBUILDERS

### OVERVIEW

It is well established that home building activity increases prospective lot and house/lot buyers' interest in a subdivision.

However, if this is your initial subdivision or you presently do not have an interest in home building, you have two good options to jump start buyer interest in your subdivision.

One method is, **"discounting the lot asking price."** As the name implies, you are exchanging a lower sale price for immediate construction and cash, it can be very advantageous. You should only offer it to an established home builder with stellar business credentials. Also, the cash from the sale can help reduce the need for borrowing and/or pay down prior borrowing.

The other method which I have used in my personal and partnership development projects is, **"fronting a lot,"** again only to an established, quality home builder prepared to immediately commence home construction.

You ask, what does **"fronting a lot"** to a home builder entail?

**In exchange for building a house, lot payment is postponed until one of the following occurs:**

A.) Upon the sale of the completed house
B.) A specific due date
C.) A specific period of time after completion of the house

**Fronting a lot has two key components for protection of the developer:**

A.) Timeline – home builder start date and dates to complete various stages of the house construction
B.) Risk Management:
   1.) Home builder selection:
      a.) Established business
      b.) Quality product
      c.) Good personal and business reputation
      d.) Strong credit history
      e.) No bankruptcy or foreclosures
      f.) No property or equipment tax liens
      g.) No lawsuits or Lis pendens
      h.) No mechanics liens
      i.) No unsatisfied judgments
      j.) Insurance coverage in place – liability and workers' compensation
      k.) No subordination by developer to a lender to the home builder

   2.) Agreement criteria:
      a.) Home builder disclosure of any other speculative homes under construction, awaiting start of construction, or completed and unsold.
      b.) Assurances home builder staff, equipment and materials will be immediately available
      c.) Notification of developer if any changes enumerated in Risk Management occurs
      d.) Penalty for failure to adhere to timeline schedule
      e.) Home builder liable for developer legal expenses to enforce any condition of the Agreement
      f.) Home builder liable for all expense of foreclosing on home builder

Both above methods by generating home construction activity in the subdivision can significantly increase prospective buyer activity and lot sales to individuals, who are the majority of purchasers in subdivisions.

Your attorney, accountant and banker should be consulted for appropriate investigations of a prospective home builder, and for preparation of an agreement between the parties.

In effect, both methods make the home builder your "partner" without the big, standard partner negative, sharing of profits.

## MONITORING HOME CONSTRUCTION

Developers of subdivisions who only sell lots and do not build the homes, need to have in place before the first lots are offered for sale, a plan for monitoring the construction of homes.

Whether selling to home builders for speculative or contract home building, or fronting lots to home builders, or selling to individual buyers who will contract with a home builder to construct their personal residence, all must be monitored to protect your investment.

**Why you ask? Home construction can have unforeseen issues, such as:**

A.) Inconsistent construction – start and stop construction is the wrong message for prospective buyers

B.) No construction for months, builder way off timeline schedule

C.) Construction not meeting the quality level stipulated

D.) Unauthorized modification to the developer approved house plan

These above events can negatively affect your subdivision value and sales rate. Monitoring is how to eliminate or reduce it. See, "Chapter 11 – Closing and Post Closing, Declaration of Covenants and Restrictions", it sets out all the criteria that you the developer envision as necessary for a successful subdivision.

Monitoring of home construction is the tool by which you, the developer can obtain the desired result home after home. Monitoring begins during the initial stages of a prospect considering a purchase by identifying the home style they wish to build. It can be photos of comparable homes or a sketch, so they can obtain the developers preliminary approval, subject to actual home plans and when required a site development plan for approval by the developer.

Thereafter it is continuous monitoring that results in the quality subdivision desired, and best profitability.

**The principal areas to be reviewed:**

A.) Location of house on lot

B.) Architectural style

C.) Square footage: house footprint area and total house area
D.) Physical samples: of roof shingles; siding; and house color
E.) Limits of tree clearing
F.) Driveway location, width, surface type
G.) Landscaping plan
H.) Sedimentation and erosion control devices
I.) Location of wells and subsurface sewage disposal system
J.) Any proposed on-site debris burial locations
K.) Accessory structures comply with restrictions.

## MARKETING SUBDIVISION

Should you market lots in-house, especially if this is your first subdivision? Marketing in-house can reduce or eliminate paying a commission on lot sales. However, sales may occur at a slower rate when not represented by a real estate professional.

Assuming you want sales as quickly as possible, unless you are also a real estate professional, hire one. Keep your eye on the main goal, selling enough lots to reduce or eliminate development debt, a good position to be in.

However, there is a possibility for some in-house sales. That possibility is with local quality home builders who buy lots and do not develop subdivisions. Find them. Contact them. You should begin contacting them, especially if no infrastructure is needed no later than when you submit your application for subdivision. If infrastructure is required for your subdivision, contact them not later than when you obtain subdivision approval. Another plus for lots first going under contract to home builders is that unlike an individual looking for a lot to build their home, builders understand that a subdivision with ongoing installation of infrastructure is a positive, not a concern, whereas individuals can be reluctant to make an offer until roads are substantially completed. The home builders win by having the choice of lots, you win by early sales with cash for your balance sheet.

For a small "mom and pop" sized subdivision, especially without road infrastructure, just shared driveways, in-house selling may be quite viable. It worked very well for me with my first two personal Connecticut subdivision developments.

Attempting marketing other than direct contact with homebuilders requires time and money. Advertising requires money, and meeting with prospects can consume a lot of your time, also you don't have the ability a realtor has to pre-qualify a prospect as a candidate for a loan if the prospect hasn't done so themselves.

When listing your lots for sale with the realtor you have selected, it should always be an Exclusive Listing, as this gives your subdivision the maximum exposure to potential buyers as it is tied to MLS (Multiple Listing Service) which connects your listing to all the other real estate firms which are members of MLS, their agents, and in particular their prospective customers.

## MEDIA INTERACTION

Developers typically do not seek out the media, but a reporter for the local newspaper may very well seek to interview you, typically approaching you when leaving a municipal meeting on your subdivision application.

Why would they be interested in your project? Generally, when they hear questions by the commissioners which might imply some issues with the subdivision, or negative comments from the audience in attendance.

Many residents although living in homes which very likely were created as part of earlier subdivisions find the status quo as being just fine, and that additional subdivisions and their future residents are viewed as a negative.

I have also been subjected while speaking privately with a reporter post hearing outside of a meeting room, to the conversation being hijacked and turned into an ad hoc free-for-all by certain members of the public who had spoken in opposition during the hearing, interjecting themselves into the conversation, an unpleasant situation. Just make sure no one is in proximity to you if you decide to speak with a reporter.

Lastly, remember to be careful with your responses if you choose to engage with a reporter, as you have no control over the content of a resultant news item.

# CHAPTER 17

## WARNINGS – BE CAUTIOUS

### OVERVIEW

This chapter's topics have no relation to each other, instead each is a different cautionary regarding the potential threat that each can visit upon your activities, you are now forewarned.

## SUBDIVISION DECLARED NULL AND VOID

There are two situations that you must closely monitor to protect your approved subdivision from disaster.

The first situation was discussed earlier in Chapter 11, you should revisit it as it bears rereading. It revolves around the deadline to file an approved subdivision, otherwise the Planning and Zoning Commission can declare your subdivision to be, "null and void;" besides your state statutes may make that action mandatory or automatic.

### We Now Discuss a Very Different Situation

How is it that a subdivision map which met the deadline for filing in the land records of a town clerk can yet become null and void?

It is due to the failure of the developer to either begin installation of the infrastructure improvements or failure to complete them, prior to the statutory deadline for completion of infrastructure, resulting in the subdivision becoming null and void. Depending upon state statutes, null and void may be automatic, or more likely require the Planning and Zoning Commission to vote on voiding its approval. In either instance a notice declaring the subdivision null and void will be recorded in the land records of the town clerk and likely the filed subdivision maps will be stamped as null and void.

The developer now has all, or a significant portion of the subdivision immediately reverted to one or more vacant land tracts, excepting for the following possibilities.

**Null and Void Subdivision – Exclusions:**

A.) Lots previously conveyed to third parties by the developer
B.) Road right-of-way if already deeded to the municipality
C.) Open space if already deeded to the designated entity, such as, a land preservation trust or home owner's association
D.) Easements deeded for utilities, fire protection facilities, etc.

If subdivision roads have not yet been conveyed to the municipality, third party owners of lots will have the right to pass and repass upon said "road," as an easement in their favor, from their lot to the nearest public road. Said subdivision "roads" would now become part of the vacant land of the developer.

Any subdivision lots or homes that have direct access to an existing public road or highway that were conveyed to third parties or are still owned by the developer are exempt from the effect of the null and void action affecting the rest of the subdivision.

**Subdividing the Vacant Land of a Null and Void Subdivision:**

Any individual, whether the original developer or another party, seeking approval to subdivide the vacant land of a null and void subdivision must make application for subdivision per the current regulations.

**However, there can be two potential problems.**

**First.** If changes to the subdivision, zoning, or inland wetlands regulations have been enacted, the subdivision design must conform to these current standards, there is **"no grandfathering"** of those regulations in effect when the now voided subdivision was approved.

**Second.** The Planning and Zoning Commission and other regulatory agencies can impose both the same conditions of the original subdivision plus additional conditions of approval.

**Note:** Verify if there were approved inland wetlands regulated activity permits, and if the approvals survive a subdivision declared null and void if a new subdivision application is submitted to the Planning and Zoning Commission. If not, then that is another regulatory application which must also comply with any changes to those regulations.

## COMMISSIONER PERSONAL AGENDA

As a developer and consultant professional land surveyor designing subdivisions and presenting applications for over 30 years before regulatory commissions, occasionally it became apparent that comments of a commission member were outside of the regulations "envelope", indicating an actual or a potential personal agenda.

Throughout the many municipalities in which I practiced, it was uncommon to have even a single member who had a professional background in land use, development, planning, engineering, etc., members were from many backgrounds other than a land use field.

A duty of the chairperson of a commission is to remind members, if necessary, to follow their regulations. Unfortunately, some chairpersons are not at times up to the task.

If this situation arises and is not corrected by the chairperson if a member is making statements, comments and asking questions outside of the regulations, it raises a concern about having an impartial decision on the application, so what should the application presenter do?

The presenter has two options to attempt to mitigate the situation before the application may be perceived unfavorably, especially if a vote on the application is a possibility at the conclusion of the presentation. Address the chairperson as to your concern regarding a member's comments/questions versus the regulations and in especially egregious situations, request the chairperson to ask the member to recuse I, or request that the commission continue the application to the next meeting.

Better yet, if the applicants' attorney is present, turn this matter over to the attorney. If not present, again request a continuation to the next meeting when the developer's attorney would attempt to resolve the situation with the commission before turning the application presentation back to the technical consultant.

## ADJOINING OWNERS ACTING IN BAD FAITH

Planning and Zoning Commissions can at times be over accommodating to property owners that adjoin a proposed subdivision who are expressing their alleged concerns that the subdivision will unfavorably affect them.

At times concerns of neighbors have a degree of merit or can be the result of not understanding development plans or technical reports. Then there are those neighbors who just want no development next to them and have no scruples about concocting issues to delay the application in hope that the developer withdraws the application or makes significant modifications in proximity to their properties.

Due to their complaints the commission may request that the application be continued to the next meeting and that the applicant, and the neighbors meet to try to resolve their concerns before the next meeting.

Unfortunately, if these property owners are just going through the motions regarding their complaints, their apparent agreement with changes agreed to by the applicant may be a mirage, likely followed at the next commission meeting with new complaints.

This is indicative of a potential cycle of requests for the developer to again meet with them before the next meeting, however their intent is not to reach a resolution, at least a reasonable one, but to either radically modify the subdivision so it is not feasible to pursue development, or to convince the commission to deny the application, they are **"acting in bad faith"**.

Infrequently in my professional practice I have had occasions where applications were targeted by adjoining property owners acting in bad faith, raising new concerns at each subsequent hearing on the application. When the commission members allowed this process to continue multiple times, the unfortunate result for the applicant was, at the minimum two or three additional months added to the application hearing process.

**What to do?** Attempt to get these property owners after meeting with them to sign a statement that the concerns they raised have been resolved and they have no further objections. Present it to the commission at the next meeting. However, there is little likelihood that they would agree to sign such a statement.

The first time I experienced what turned out to be neighbors acting in bad faith regarding a client's application, the commission encouraged both sides to meet post hearing to discuss and resolve their concerns. This was done but at the next commission meeting the property owners raised new concerns and the hearing was again continued, and again we met with them, supposedly resolving these new concerns.

However, at the next hearing the spokesperson for the neighbors unexpectedly rose and again began to raise new concerns, it was then obvious to me that they were untrustworthy and there was no end to them continuing to raise new objections at future hearings. I broke hearing procedure interrupting the spokesperson, I stated to the commission that we had once again been assured by the neighbors that all concerns were addressed. I continued that the applicant had bent over backwards to accommodate them at all prior post hearing meetings and that their present attempt at further new alleged concerns makes it clear that they were acting **"in bad faith."** With that statement to objecting neighbor returned to his seat, I then requested that the commission immediately close the hearing on our application and vote to approve it. Which the commission did. So be careful about being stringed along by "bad faith actors."

# MONITOR FOR REGULATION CHANGES

## OVERVIEW

I cannot stress the importance of the following advice.

Beginning with the location of a potential property to subdivide and continuing until the application to subdivide has been accepted as complete by the Planning and Zoning Commission, thereby locking the application into being considered per the present regulations, you must monitor the zoning and subdivision regulations for proposed changes. Your consultants can determine whether any proposed change has a negative impact on the design, lot yield, or development costs of the subdivision and whether there is a way to moderate its impact.

**Sources to monitor – potential changes to regulations:**

A.) Municipal land use staff

B.) Staff of other municipal departments whose regulations may also apply to subdivisions

C.) Websites of the above agencies, in particular meeting agendas and minutes of meetings

D.) The local newspaper legal notices of upcoming meetings, and articles by its governmental affairs reporter about preliminary discussions to amend regulations.

What can be done if a proposed regulation change that negatively impacts your proposed subdivision will become effective prior to your application for subdivision being submitted for acceptance by the Planning and Zoning Commission under the existing regulations?

**Potential options to mitigate changes:**

A.) Oppose the regulation change at its public hearing:

1.) Individually, represented by your land use attorney

2.) Jointly, with other landowners, preferably not developers, ideally with a land use attorney.

B.) If the change is approved, appeal the approval to Superior Court seeking its denial. At the minimum it will delay the effective date of the regulation, giving you additional time that may allow for the completion of your subdivision design and its application submission under the existing regulations.

C.) Divide your subdivision into sections so that the design time for the initial section is reduced, potentially allowing for this section of the property to be accepted by the Planning and Zoning Commission under the existing regulations. Repeat this for as many sections as possible while your appeal is pending.

D.) Further delay the effective date of the regulation change if the decision of Superior Court is not favorable by appealing the decision to the next higher court, the Appellate Court, giving you additional time to hopefully submit more sections or even the entire subdivision under the existing regulations.

## EMINENT DOMAIN

### OVERVIEW

Eminent domain is the power of government to expropriate private property against the wishes of the owner for public use, with payment of compensation. All political levels of government, federal, state, county, and municipal have the power of eminent domain.

The good news is that it is not common, especially in what can be described as towns where much of the single-family residential subdivision development is taking place or will be in years ahead.

During my thirty plus years as a consultant designer of subdivisions only one of my clients experienced eminent domain, it resulted in a nasty financial bite, though it seems to me that it was self-induced.

A property had been sized by a federal agency due the owner's involvement in drug trafficking. It was offered as per regulation starting first with federal entities and if no interest working down through each lower level of government jurisdiction until the last level, municipal government. If no government entity had interest in acquiring a property, it would finally be offered to the public by bid or auction. That is how my clients obtained it, then hiring my firm to design a residential subdivision.

Shortly after we began work our clients were approached by the municipal government, the Town of Clinton, it had a change of interest in the property and now wished to acquire it from them. The town offered the same money that our clients paid for the property plus a minimal additional amount for closing expenses.

They refused the offer, and the town then began eminent domain proceedings for the purpose of building a public school on the property.

Our clients instructed us to work as quickly as possible to complete the design and submit a subdivision application to the Planning and Zoning Commission, under their theory that its approval would demonstrate a significant increase in value above what they had paid, and that the town would then need to pay that amount if it wanted to acquire the property.

Unfortunately, though I don't recall the specifics of the court's determination other than that it sustained the eminent domain claim of the town and awarded it the property, with the compensation to my clients being the exact amount of money that they had paid to acquire the property.

So, they wasted a substantial amount of money on my consultant fees, their attorney, plus tall the time and effort that could have been invested in a non-controversial property.

You are now well advised to beware of a property with any smell of possible eminent domain potential.

## ERRONEROUS EFFECTIVE DATE OF REGULATIONS

### OVERVIEW

I had designed a residential subdivision in the Town of Madison beginning with a "split-by-right" of the property. State statutes permitted the creation of one lot, the "split-by-right," after the initial adoption of subdivision regulations, avoiding those regulations and only needing to comply with the zoning standards. This gave the property owner a quicker sale of the lot, and if a developer is the buyer, reduction of open space and possibly other benefits. In this instance the lot was to be retained by the sellers of the property as it was their personal residence. The subdivision had been approved, and the closing was imminent.

I was in the process of researching the land records of the town clerk for a property survey elsewhere in town prior to commencing field work, when I found a subdivision map of a property that adjoined my client's property. What caught my immediate attention was the 1951 date of approval and endorsement of the subdivision map by the chairperson of the Planning and Zoning Commission. This was subdivision map #3 as stamped by the Town Clerk's office. Also in the file drawer were subdivision maps #1 and #2, both dated and approved in 1950.

The problem was that the published Madison Subdivision Regulations cited an effective date in 1953 which all zoning officers had represented for years as the date of the initial subdivision regulations. I informed the current zoning officer of my discovery to no avail. After he left a clerk caught my attention and went through what appeared to be very old documents and quietly brought over a copy of Subdivision Regulations dated in 1950, it consisted of all of six pages.

So, you ask how did this interesting uncovering of regulation history affect the subdivision I initially mentioned above, and which my client's attorney was about to close? It turned out the adjoining lot to my client's seller, her sister, was initially also part of the family property. The sister's lot was conveyed out of the family property prior to 1953, so I had dismissed it as having any negative bearing on a "split-by-right" with respect to the current form of the property to create the seller's proposed house lot. However, as the sister's lot had been conveyed out post 1950 it made the first sister's lot the actual "split-by-right" lot, not the current sellers proposed residence lot.

**Fast stop**. The outcome was that the closing was postponed, and we returned to the Planning and Zoning Commission with a revised subdivision map incorporating the sellers house lot as part of the subdivision.

This was a once in a career event, but you or your consultant may want to double check the effective date of the original subdivision regulations if a "split-by-right" is being considered for your subdivision.

# APPENDIX

The following forms and mapping are typical of those used in many Connecticut municipalities for the analysis and investigation of land in determining its development potential, and for application to regulatory agencies for approval of residential subdivisions.

The length and detail of the above can vary significantly between municipalities, those included are representative of the purpose of each form type.

| FOR OFFICE USE ONLY |
|---|
| Date Entered: |
| Application ID # |

Guilford Planning and Zoning Commission
Town Hall South- 50 Boston Street- Guilford CT 06437
T: 203-453-8039 F: 203-453-8034

**APPLICATION FOR SUBDIVISION/ RE-SUBDIVISION APPROVAL**
**Submit one (1) original and six (6) Copies SEND DIGITAL PDF TO planning.zoning@ci.guilford.ct.us**

Date: ______________________ **SUBDIVISION [ ]** **RE-SUBDIVISION [ ] (select one)**

Application is hereby made for the approval of a subdivision/re-subdivision plan entitled:
__________________________________________

Location: __________________________________________
Assessors Map #:______________ Lot:______________ Zone District: ______________

Applicant's Name:__________________________________________
Address:__________________________________________
__________________________________________
__________________________________________
Telephone:______________________
Fax:______________________
E-mail:______________________

Property Owner (if different from applicant): ______________________
Address:
__________________________________________
__________________________________________
Telephone: ______________________

Surveyor or Engineer's Name:______________________
Address: __________________________________________
__________________________________________
__________________________________________
Telephone:______________________

Total Area of Subdivision/ReSubdivision:______________ Area of Section: ______________
Total # of Lots:______________ # of lots in Section: ______________
Describe existing structures, if any: ______________________
Is there any water source within or contiguous to the property? ☐ Yes ☐ No Name if known ________
List any potential hazards within or contiguous to the property (steep cliffs, easements for high-pressure gas lines, power transmission lines, etc.) ______________________
__________________________________________
Does owner of record own or have any interest in a partnership or corporation owning abutting property?
☐Yes☐ No
Has any zoning variance been granted concerning this property? ☐Yes (Attach copy of letter) ☐No
Is there a proposed new street or improvement of existing street? ☐New ☐Existing improvement
If so, are copies of the road profile(s) submitted? ☐Yes ☐No
Are copies of drainage plan(s) submitted? ☐Yes ☐No
Are you aware that the Regulations require submission of the Town Engineer's and Director of Health's report before final approval can be granted? ☐Yes ☐No

If not owner of record, has applicant been legally authorized to act as agent for the owner? ☐Yes ☐No

If applicant is not the owner of record at the time of application submission, this form must be signed by the owner, or a letter authorizing the applicant to act as lawful agent of the owner must accompany this application. (§272-13A of the subdivision regulations).

Signed:_________________________ _________________________

Applicant Owner

Date: _________________________ _________________________

**Low Impact Development Zoning and Subdivision Code Amendments**

Amend Zoning Code, Article IX Site Plan Review by adding the following;

§273-75 General Standards

R. Low Impact Development. Applicants for Site Plan review are encouraged to practice low impact development as described in "Guidance Document for Low Impact Development Best Management Practices", dated 12/15/09 and as it may be amended. Applicants shall complete "A Check List to Guide Low Impact Development Best Management Practices."

**GUIDANCE DOCUMENT FOR LOW IMPACT DEVELOPMENT BEST MANAGEMENT PRACTICES FOR GUILFORD March 11, 2010**

## INTRODUCTION

Over the past 30 years, Guilford has seen an increase in balancing environmental conservation with human needs, community growth and land use practices. Low Impact Development is an approach to the use of land which utilizes a variety of innovative approaches to site planning, conservation design and storm water management. Overall, the goal of Low Impact Development is to make the fewest changes to the environment consistent with zero increase in storm water runoff, environmental protection and economic considerations.

As a result of this approach, studies have shown that construction costs are reduced[1], local property values are likely to rise[2], tax revenues increase and compliance with wetlands and other resource protection regulations is easier[3].

Guilford's Storm Water Management regulations (adopted in 2005) require storm water management plans to be consistent with the latest version of Connecticut's Storm Water Quality Manual. In this document, Section 4 describes Low Impact Development (LID) Site Planning and Management Practices. Additional guidance is described in "The Practice of Low Impact Development" by the US Department of Housing and Urban Development Office of Policy Development and Research, dated July 2003.

LID Planning and Design Practices include Site Planning, Erosion and Sediment Control, Storm Water Management and Landscape Design principles. To highlight those LID Management Practices expected in Guilford, the following principles are suggested for review by designers and developers. The attached checklist is intended for designers and developers to complete in order to provide the Planning and Zoning Commission and staff an overview of the developer's efforts to protect natural resources wherever reasonable on any given site.

## SITE PLANNING CONSIDERATIONS

Environmentally sensitive development is a prime importance in Guilford, as is preservation of those elements which represent the Town's historic and cultural heritage. A visually appealing site plan which will stabilize and/ or increase property values and encourage sustainable development and energy efficient design are important elements to be included in a Site Plan application wherever possible.

Site Plans should also respect unique natural and historic features such as stone walls and public view sheds. As a result of this approach to site planning, more aesthetically pleasing and naturally attractive landscapes, more pedestrian friendly neighborhoods, more open space for recreation, and safer residential streets can be expected[4].

Site planning can be divided into a four step process.

1. Identification of Natural Resources

2. Locating buildings outside the natural resource area wherever possible

3. Lay out streets, driveways, parking areas and trails.

4. Creation of lot lines.

Step1. Identification of Natural Resources

An initial site assessment is conducted to determine the location of all natural resources on a given site. These resources shall include wetlands, coastal resources, meadows, steep slopes, soil types, mature forest, significant trees, riparian corridors, wildlife corridors, view sheds, and the location of any endanger species. Most of these elements have already been identified in Guilford's 2005 Natural Resource Inventory and Assessment (NRIA) and they are illustrated in the NRIA Map Atlas. Other natural resource references are identified in Table 1.

After a document review of the site has been performed, a field survey should be conducted to locate hydrologic features such as streams, wetlands, floodplains and existing natural surface water drainage patterns. Once wetlands features have been identified, a surveyor needs to locate them on a site plan along with features such as site topography, limits of vegetation, exposed ledge and stone walls. Additional items required on a site plan are listed on the attached Low Impact Design Best Management Practices check list and in Table 1.

Step 2.Locating buildings outside the natural resource areas wherever possible

As a result of these initial steps, a site plan can be created showing areas of the site best suited for development and areas of the site that should be conserved. The developable areas are those locations on the site which will least disturb the natural resources and have the fewest regulator and zoning concerns. It may be advisable to cluster the development into one area of the site or into several smaller clusters that protect the site's natural features.

Conservation lands should include both inland and tidal wetlands, areas within the "A", "AE", or "V" flood zone as depicted on the flood Hazard Boundary Map or Flood Insurance Rate Map, steep slopes in excess of 25 percent (10 feet vertical in less than 40 feet horizontal), areas adjacent to open space, historic features such as stone walls, natural features such as fields, mature trees and forest, public view sheds, wildlife corridors, and site areas that contain threatened or endangered species.

Step 3. Lay out streets, driveways, parking areas and trails

The lay out of streets, driveways, and parking areas should be designed after the site analysis. These features should be laid out in a way that minimizes their overall length and width and cutting and filling to conform to natural contours. Shared parking and driveways need to be considered. Streets and driveways should conform to natural land formations in order to reduce impact on the natural resources where possible.

Step 4. Draw in the lot lines

Once the above steps have been completed, the lot lines (if any) can be drawn based on the location of buildings, driveways, septic systems, and wells. Due to the clustering of development, developers may be able to take advantage of an Open Space Subdivision or a Planned Residential Development.

**EROSION AND SEDIMENT CONTROL**

Erosion and storm water drainage plans should utilize natural topography wherever possible. To reduce erosion of exposed soils and prevent sedimentation of wetlands, water bodies and other sensitive areas, land disturbance should be minimized to the area necessary for construction. Proposed development projects on a previously undeveloped site should minimize clearing and grading, especially in areas of steep slopes, erosion-prone soils and sensitive vegetation. For redevelopment projects, the site plan should concentrate development on previously disturbed areas to the extent possible. Vegetation outside immediate construction areas should remain undisturbed. Any disturbed areas should be replanted or heavily mulched. Erosion and sedimentation control plans shall be constructed in accordance with The Town of Guilford Subdivision and Zoning Codes using principles outlined in the Connecticut Guidelines for Soil Erosion Sediment Control (2002), as the same maybe revised.

**STORMWATER MANAGEMENT**

Guilford's stormwater management regulations are designed to protect local and regional wetlands and water bodies, Long Island Sound and its tributaries from non-point sources of pollution and to maximize groundwater recharge on site. The goal of LID stormwater management is to mimic pre-development hydrologic conditions by utilizing natural topography and soils to detain, retain, percolate and evaporate source and use natural treatment systems instead of a centralized collection point. Non-structural stormwater management systems should be used, in part or in whole, only if the applicant can demonstrate that other systems are not feasible due to site conditions.

**LANDSCAPE DESIGN**

Demand for irrigation should be minimized and groundwater recharge from landscaped areas should be maximized to the extent possible. To reduce proliferation of invasive species, native plants should be used wherever possible. All disturbed areas should be replanted or mulched in accordance to the Erosion and Sedimentation Control plan. Plants on the 2004 Connecticut DEP Invasive Plant List (as the same maybe revised) should not be used.

The existing vegetation outside the immediate construction area should remain undisturbed. Significant existing trees within the proposed development area should be preserved where possible as per the following caliper size thresholds related to species:

- 4-6" for small trees such as dogwood and redbud
- 8-10" for medium species such as sassafras, cherry and water beech
- 12-14" for slow growing hardwoods (oak, maple, ash)
- 15-18" for fast growers such as tulip poplar, sycamore and conifers[5]

As a result of these practices, forests, wetlands, and wildlife habitat would be preserved.

**Definitions:**

Permanent Erosion & Sedimentation Control Measures- Long term devices placed, constructed on or applied to the landscape that prevents or curb the detachment of soil, the movement of water and or the deposition of sediment. Examples include detention basins, grass swales, level spreaders, and vegetation.

Steep slopes- A steep slope has a grade of more than 25% and an area of 1,000 square feet or more. The grade is measured along a line perpendicular to the lot contours established at intervals not exceeding two feet.

View Shed- Scenic views into and from the site and any other features that contribute to the landscape character of the property. Examples include meadows, notable trees ridgelines, rock outcrops, stonewalls, beaches and dunes, Long Island Sound and its tributaries.

Stormwater Detention- Control measures that temporarily holds and gradually releases a volume of stormwater runoff to attenuate and delay stormwater runoff peaks.

Stormwater Best Management Practices- practices designed to mitigate the effects of stormwater runoff to attenuate flooding, reduce erosion, and reduce pollution.

**Reference:**


1. Reducing Stormwater Costs through Low Impact Development (LID), Strategies and Practices, EPA Publication number 841-F07-006, December 2007
2. The Economic Value of Open Space: A review and Synthesis, CJ Fausold and RJ Lilieholm, Environmental Management Volume 23 (3):307-320,1999
3. The Practice of Low Impact Development by the U.S. Department of Housing and Urban Development, July.
4. 2004 Connecticut Stormwater Quality Manual prepared by the Connecticut Department of Environmental Protection.
5. Conservation Subdivision Design: A Brief Overview by Randall Arendt, FRTPI, ASLS (Hon.)


Table 1
LID/BMP Resource Requirements and Resources

| **Natural Resource Regulatory Requirements** | | | **Natural Resource Reference Sources** | |
|---|---|---|---|---|
| **Natural Resource Elements** | **PZC Site Plan map reqt.** | **Inland Wetlands app** | **Natural Resource Inventory** | **Other References** |
| Contours and slopes >25% | Already required | #5 | | Site survey already required |
| Watercourse boundaries @100' | Already required | #6 | | Site survey already required |
| Soil mapping | | #16.D | Map A-4 Prime soils | USDA map/ wetland soils |
| Wetlands and watercourses | | IWC jurisdiction | Map J-2 | IWC regulations –Appx A |
| Stone walls | Already required | | | Site survey already |

| | | | | |
|---|---|---|---|---|
| | | | | required |
| Ledge and rock outcroppings | Often already included | | | Site survey required |
| Logging roads and trails | Often already included | | | Site survey required |
| Flood hazard areas | | | Map C-2 | FEMA maps |
| Aquifers and watersheds | | | Map C-1 for watersheds | Zoning map for aquifers |
| Natural drainage areas-swales | | #9A (for regulated area only) | | Inferred from contours |
| Impervious surface % whole site | Commercial and Industrial Zones VLB & proposed CAM regs | | Map of 10% VLBs at build out | Storm water regs |
| Rare and endangered species | | | Map J-3 and THS wall map | CT DEP NDDB maps |
| Significant forests & Grasslands | | | Map J-1 | Property survey already reqd |
| Significant Natural Resource Areas (SNRAs) | | | Map J-6 | |
| Wildlife movement corridors | | | Map J-4 | CT DEP NDDB maps |
| Viewsheds | Cam Regulations Only | | Section G, Map G Appx G1&2 | Site survey required |
| Significant trees (in proposed development area only) | | | | See definitions in BMP text Site survey required |
| Contiguity of site with protected open space, unbuilt land, wetlands & ridgelines | | | | USGS, NRI Map H-3, GIS plus aerial photos |

## A CHECK LIST TO GUIDE LOW IMPACT DEVELOPMENT – BEST MANAGEMENT PRACTICES

Date: ______________________________

Assessor Map No. ______________________________ Lot No. ____________________

Location of Property: ______________________________________________

Applicant: ______________________________________________________

Items listed below should be considered by developers in the creation of site plans. Due to individual site constraints not all items will apply to each individual property. CHECK ALL ITEMS THAT HAVE BEEN ADDRESSED IN THE SITE PLAN APPLICATION. Applicants should indicate by writing Yes, No, or N/A (not applicable). Additional comments are to be attached on a separate sheet of paper with project name and address.

### A. SITE PLAN CONSIDERATIONS

| **1. Site Assessment of Natural Resources** | **Applicant** | **Staff Comments** |
|---|---|---|
| a. Natural Resources and constraints have been indicated and are identified on the plans (wetlands, rivers, streams, flood hazard zones, meadows, agricultural land, tree lines, slopes [2 foot contours], soil types, exposed ledge & stone walls). | | |
| b. Is the property shown on the latest copy of CT DEP State and Federal Listed Species and Significant Natural Communities Map as property listed in the Natural Diversity Data Base (NDDB)? If yes, provide a copy of the CT-DEP NDDB request form and CT-DEP reply letter. | | |
| c. Development is designed to avoid critical coastal resources, water courses, wetlands and steep slopes. | | |
| d. Soils Suitable for septic & stormwater infiltration have been identified | | |

| | | |
|---|---|---|
| e. Natural existing drainage patterns have been delineated on the plan and are proposed to be preserved or impacts minimized. | | |
| f. Significant trees/ tree clusters in proposed development areas have been identified. Removal avoided and or protection in conservation easement suggested. (See guidance document). | | |
| g. View sheds have been recognized/ maximized | | |
| h. A copy of the latest USGS Quad map along with an aerial photograph showing the site and adjacent properties is attached. | | |

| 2. Preservation of Open Space | Applicant | Staff Comments |
|---|---|---|
| a. An open space subdivision or planned residential development (PRD) has been considered. | | |
| b. Open space/ common areas are delineated. | | |
| c. Open space is retained in a natural condition. | | |
| d. Proposed open space is located adjacent to open space areas, trail systems, and / or wild life corridors. ( See Town of Guilford Natural Resource Inventory) | | |
| e. Coastal Public access should be evaluated for properties with non water-dependent uses on waterfront sites. | | |
| f. Street line setbacks are minimized to reduce impervious surface and to optimize open space. | | |

| 3. Minimization of Land Disturbance | Applicant | Staff Comments |
|---|---|---|
| a. The proposed building is located where development can occur with the least environmental impact. | | |
| b. Buildings designed for maximum solar gain. (Window exposure, are oriented to the sun for maximum energy efficiency). | | |
| c. Clustered development has been considered. | | |
| d. Disturbance areas have been delineated to avoid unnecessary clearing or grading, | | |
| e. Sanitary systems should be setback from water bodies to maximum extent possible. | | |
| f. Native Vegetation outside the immediate construction areas remains undisturbed or will be restored. | | |

| 4. Street and Driveway Sizes | Applicant | Staff Comments |
|---|---|---|
| a. The design provides an efficient layout to minimize the overall length and width of streets. | | |
| b. Roadways and driveways conform to natural land formations. | | |
| c. Design features to reduce impervious surfaces such as shared parking & Driveways have been considered. | | |
| d. Proposed drainage systems utilize existing topography. | | |

### B. EROSION AND SEDIMENT CONTROL

| EROSION AND SEDIMENT CONTROL | Applicant | Staff Comments |
|---|---|---|
| a. Erosion and Sedimentation control plan is designed in accordance to Guilford Subdivision and Zoning Regulations. | | |
| b. Permanent erosion control measures are to be utilized. | | |
| c. Development does not create steep slopes subject to erosion | | |
| d. Vegetated buffers are provided for riparian areas, intermittent streams, and wetlands. | | |
| e. Cleared areas will be replanted and/ or heavily mulched. | | |

### C. MANAGING STORMWATER

| MANAGING STORMWATER | Applicant | Staff Comments |
|---|---|---|
| a. Efforts have been made to retain or infiltrate water on site. | | |

| | | |
|---|---|---|
| b. Outfalls are stabilized and receiving streams are protected from sediment scour potential velocity. | | |
| c. Level spreaders or dispersed flow methods are used only where natural dispersal is not possible | | |
| d. Maximum use is made of vegetated ditches/ swales, especially along driveways, parking areas and roads. | | |
| e. Cul-de-sacs include a landscape island for bio-retention. | | |
| f. Sheet flow is used to the maximum extent possible to avoid concentrating runoff. | | |
| g. Rooftop drainage is discharged into bio-retention areas or rain gardens. | | |
| h. Innovations like collecting/ reusing rainwater, green roofs, or porous pavement have been considered. | | |
| i. Grass swales are used beside roads instead of curbs and gutters. | | |
| j. Parking medians are designed for bio-retention to allow infiltration. | | |
| k. Infiltration structures have been included –e.g. drywells and infiltration trenches. | | |
| l. Best Management Practices to provide water quality treatment to remove existing and expected pollutants generated to be the proposed use. | | |
| m. Impervious surfaces are disconnected and stormwater is treated locally. | | |
| n. Proposed construction of the storm water management system is designed in compliance with the Guilford Town Codes and Connecticut Stormwater Manuel. | | |
| o. Onsite soil infiltration/ permeability has been measured. | | |
| p. Onsite soils are suitable for stormwater detention/ infiltration. | | |
| q. Sufficient areas of infiltration (if present) are being utilized to maximize onsite stormwater retention. | | |

**D. LANDSCAPE PLAN**

| **LANDSCAPE PLAN** | **Applicant** | **Staff Comments** |
|---|---|---|
| a. Clearing and grading have been minimized. | | |
| b. Irrigation with automatic sensors have been considered. | | |
| c. Landscaped areas retain water such as in water gardens, vegetated swales, etc. | | |
| d. Habitat-enhancing native plant species are used. | | |
| e. Species appropriate to soil, site, wetlands and microclimate conditions have been considered. | | |
| f. Indigenous plants suitable for vegetated buffers, stream corridors and wetlands are included. | | |
| g. Plants on the 2004 CT DEP Invasive Plant List are not included in the landscape design plan. | | |
| h. Invasive species removal and maintenance control plan has been considered. | | |
| i. Underground utilities have been considered. | | |

Date of Submission ______________ Date of Receipt __________

Fee ___________ Date Paid ___________

GUILFORD INLAND WETLANDS COMMISSION
APPLICATION FOR
INLAND WETLANDS AND WATER COURSES ACT – PUBLIC ACT 155

Submit FOUR copies of application and accompanying documents

1. Location of property: ______________________________________________

   Assessor's Map # _______ Lot # _______ Zone: _______

| | |
|---|---|
| Print Applicant's Name | Print Owner's Name |
| Applicant's Address | Owner's Address |
| Applicant's Phone Number | Owner's Phone Number |
| Applicant's Fax Number | Owner's Fax Number |
| Applicant's E-mail | Owner's E-mail |

2. THIS APPLICATION IS FOR:

☐ Permit to conduct regulated activity
☐ After the Fact regulated activity
☐ Site Plan Referral
☐ Special Permits/Exceptions/Exemptions
☐ Subdivision Referral
☐ Amend regulations
☐ Boundary clarification
☐ Renewal/Modification/Extension of Permit/Transfers
☐ Permitted Use As Of Right
☐ Non Regulated Use

☐ Significant Activity
☐ No Regulated Activity
☐ No Regulated Activity
Section to be amended

3. Description of Project:

4. Description of Regulated Activity:

5. General Information:

Total area of site: _____________ Upland review area to be altered: _____________

Wetland area to be altered: ________ Watercourse area to be altered: ______________

Vernal Pool Review Area to be altered: ______________

6. Applicant's interest in the land: ________________________________________

7. Additional Information: All of the following may require notification or application for permit to other municipal, state, and/or federal agencies. This is the sole responsibility of the applicant or agent.

Check those that apply:

- ☐ Any portion of the property on which the regulated activity is proposed is located within five hundred (500) feet of an adjoining municipality; or traffic, sewer, water runoff and/or water drainage will impact an adjoining municipality. (See Section 7.6 of the regulations)
- ☐ The property is within a water company watershed or aquifer protection zone and a copy of the letter notifying the proper water company of the application is enclosed.
- ☐ The property is within a floodplain or floodway
- ☐ The property contains tidal wetlands regulated by the CT DEP (See Section 5 of the regulations)
- ☐ The property contains rivers or watercourses regulated by the Army Corps of Engineers
- ☐ The property contains conservation restriction and/or preservation restriction

8. This application shall also include:
   - A map showing: geographical location of the property; inland wetlands and watercourses boundaries marked with flag numbers; areas of wetlands and watercourses and upland review area disturbances; soil types; and vegetation. (see attached checklist)
   - A site plan showing existing and proposed conditions in relation to wetlands and watercourses. (see attached checklist)
   - Alternatives considered and reasons why the proposed activity was chosen.
   - Names and addresses of adjacent property owners
   - Any other information the Commission deems necessary to the understanding of the proposed activity.

**If the proposed activity involves a significant activity, additional information may be required. (See Section 7.5 of the regulations)**

This application gives the Commission and its agents authority to inspect the property at reasonable times, both before and after a final decision has been issued.

The applicant warrants the truth of all statements contained herein and in all supporting documents according to the best of his/her knowledge and belief.

The applicant understands that this application is to be considered complete only when all information and documents required by the Guilford Inland Wetlands Commission have been submitted.

______________________________ ______________________________

Applicant's Signature & Date Owner's Signature & Date

Please attach a sheet listing any and all additional property owners and letters of authorization from each.

Sheet attached with additional property owners

Letter(s) of authorization from additional property owners attached

Contact person/agent other than applicant: ______________________________

Contact Person's Address

Phone Number: ____________________ Fax Number: ____________________

E-mail: __________________________

Site Plan and Environmental Information

The applicant shall submit a map or maps and such information concerning the proposed regulated activity(ies) as the Guilford Inland Wetlands Commission indicates below:

1. Sheet Sizes

   A. ☐ 8.5" x 11" or multiples thereof
   B. ☐ 24" x 36" or multiples thereof

2. Graphic scale for site plan information

| | Scale Suggested | Information required Outside regulated area (List) |
|---|---|---|
| A. ☐ Regulated area | 1" = 40' | |
| B. ☐ Area directly involved in regulated activity | 1" = 40' | |
| C. ☐ Property boundaries | 1" = 200' min | |
| D. ☐ Additional Area _______ ' in diameter | 1" = 200' min | |

3. ☐ North Arrow

4. Title block in lower right corner of sheet showing:

   A. ☐ Name of Project
   B. ☐ Name of owner / applicant and / or developer
   C. ☐ Date and subsequent date of revisions
   D. ☐ Legible signature of person responsible for drawing plan. Professional's certification of the plan shall be appropriate to nature of activities proposed. Such site information about the proposed uses or effect of the regulated area must be certified by a licensed land surveyor, professional engineer, professional architect, or professional landscape architect; any of which must be registered in the State of Connecticut.
   E. ☐ Any proposed on-site sewage disposal system shall be certified by a registered sanitary engineer.

5. ☐ Inland wetland and watercourse boundaries marked with flag numbers, as defined in Section 2 of these regulations, and in Section 4 of Public Act 155.

6. ☐ Boundaries and symbol of soil mapping unit (s).

7. ☐ Site areas of permit and designation of each activity.

8. ☐ Existing and proposed buildings or other structures.
   A. ☐ Location
   B. ☐ Floor elevation

9. ☐ Location, size and composition of sidewalks, off-street parking and loading areas, including driveway entrances and exits, traffic islands and barriers.

   A. ☐ Percent of regulated area to be covered with impermeable surface.

10. ☐ Location of tree islands, shrubs and other significant vegetation, both existing and proposed.

11. ☐ Source of water supply.

12. ☐ Proposed method of sewage disposal. Proposed design and specifications of on-site sewage disposal system certified by a sanitary engineer.

13. ☐ Design of existing and proposed storm drainage system including elevations by contour at not less than five foot intervals. Additional details may be required.

14. ☐ Proposed grading by not less than five foot contours of any material to be moved. Additional details may be required.

15. ☐ Location of all percolation pits, test pits and observation holes and wells.

16. ☐ Physical Data
   A. ☐ Material to be deposited and / or excavated

      1. ☐ Area
      2. ☐ Volume
      3. ☐ Physical composition (texture, components) of material to be deposited
      4. ☐ Chemical composition of all toxic materials
      5. ☐ Potential chemical reactions of deposited materials yielding toxic products or concentrations of products
      6. ☐ Final height of filled area above seasonal high water table
      7. ☐ Texture and composition of soil left after excavation
      8. ☐ Slope of excavation
      9. ☐ Depth to water table or water level if inundated after excavation

17. ☐ Watercourse Data
   A. ☐ Open water characteristics
      I. ☐ Size of ponds or lakes
      II. ☐ Depth and, if possible, volume of water

   B. ☐ Stream characteristics
      I. ☐ intermittent or continual flow

   C. ☐ Vernal Pools
   D. ☐ Known flood levels to be indicated on map

E. ☐ Discharges, if any.
I. ☐ Type
II. ☐ Frequency and volume
III. ☐ Chemical composition

F. ☐ Creation of new water bodies

18. ☐ Biological Data

| | % of Regulated Area | Dominant Species |
|---|---|---|
| A. ☐ Trees | | |
| B. ☐ Shrubs | | |
| C. ☐ Grasses, weeds, etc. | | |
| D. ☐ Aquatic | | |
| E. ☐ Pasture | | |
| F. ☐ Cultivated Area | | |

19. ☐ Probable effects of changes on:
A. ☐ Vegetation
B. ☐ Wildlife

20. ☐ Measures to protect regulated area from:
A. ☐ Erosion and sedimentation
B. ☐ Leaching and pollutants
C. ☐ Direct discharge of pollutants
D. ☐ Increased flooding and surface runoff hazards

21. ☐ Other site information as the Guilford Inland Wetlands Commission determines necessary to meet the objectives of the Regulations and Public Act 155. (List)

22. ☐ Proposed Planting Plan
A. ☐ Disturbed Wetlands / Buffer Area
B. ☐ Grading Plan / Erosion Control Planting
C. ☐ Type and number of plants proposed
1. ☐ Time proposed to ensure survival of plantings

23. ☐ Location of erosion control measures / silt fencing / hay bales.

24. ☐ Proposed wetland(s) mitigation plan(s).

**Watershed or Aquifer Area Project Notification Form**

**REQUIREMENT:**

Within seven days of filing, all applicants before a municipal Zoning Commission, Planning and Zoning Commission, Zoning Board of Appeals or Inland Wetlands Commission for any project located within a public water supply aquifer or watershed area are reguired by Public Act No. 06-53 of the CT General Statutes to notify The Commissioner of Public Health and the project area Water Company of the proposed project by providing the following information.

To determine if your project falls within a public water supply aquifer or watershed area visit the appropriate town hall and look at their *Public Drinking Water Source Protection Areas* map. If your project falls completely within or contain any part of a public water supply aquifer or watershed you are required to complete the following information.

**Note: You will need information obtained from the *Public Drinking Water Source Protection Areas* map located in the appropriate town hall to complete this form.**

---

**Step 1:** Have you already notified the CT Department of Public Health (CTDPH) of this project?

☐ No, Go to Step 2

☐ Yes, I have notified DPH under a different project name - Complete steps 4-6

☐ Yes, same name different year - Notification Year ______ Complete steps 4-6

**Step 2:**

1. Name of public water supply aquifer your project lies within: ______
2. Name of the public water supply watershed your project lies within: ______
3. Public Water Supply Identification number (PWSID) for the water utility: CT ______

**Step 3:** For 1-5 Check all that apply

1. My project is proposing:

☐ Industrial use; ☐ Commercial use; ☐ Agricultural use; ☐ Residential use;

☐ Recreational use; ☐ Transportation improvements; ☐ Institutional (school, hospital, nursing home, etc.);

☐ Quarry/Mining; ☐ Zone Change, Please Describe: ______

☐ Other, Please describe: ______

2. The total acreage of my project is:

☐ Less than or equal to 5 acres ☐ Greater than 5 acres

3. My project site contains, abuts or is within 50 feet of a:

☐ Wetland; ☐ Stream; ☐ River; ☐ Pond or Lake

4. Existing use of my project site is:

☐ Grassland/meadow; ☐ Forested; ☐ Agricultural; ☐ Transportation; ☐ Institutional (school, hospital, nursing home, etc.); ☐ Residential; ☐ Commercial; ☐ Industrial; ☐ Recreational; ☐ Quarry/Mining

☐ Other Please Describe: 

5. My project will utilize:

☐ septic system; ☐ existing public sewer; ☐ new public sewer; ☐ agricultural waste facility;

☐ existing private well; ☐ new private well; ☐ existing public water supply;

☐ new public water supply, if new have you applied for a certificate of public convenience and necessity from DPH? ☐ Yes ☐ No

6. My project will contain this percentage of built up area (buildings, parking, road/driveway, pool): ☐ Less than or equal to 20% ☐ Greater than 20% to 50% ☐ Greater than 50%

**Step: 4** Applicants Contact Information:

Name: 

E-mail address: 

Telephone: 

Fax number: 

**Step 5:** Please provide the following if available:

Project name: 

Project site address: 

Town: 

Project site nearest intersection: 

Project site latitude and longitude: 

**E-mail completed form to dph.swpmail@ct.gov**

| | |
|---|---|
| APP # | |
| PERMIT # | |

Fee - $50.00

## TOWN OF GUILFORD HEALTH DEPARTMENT
## APPLICATION FOR SITE INVESTIGATION/ SOIL TESTING

**Location:** **Map:** **Lot:** **UID#**

**Property Owner** **Owner's Phone:**

**Property Owner Address:** **Email:**

**Applicant:** **License #** **CID #**

**Applicant's Address:**

**Phone:** **Cell:** **Email:**

Date: ______________ **DEEP TEST PITS DATA/SOIL DESCRIPTIONS**

| TEST PIT: | | TEST PIT: | | TEST PIT: | | TEST PIT: | |
|---|---|---|---|---|---|---|---|
| | | | | | | | |
| Mottles: | GW: | Mottles: | GW: | Mottles: | GW: | Mottles: | GW: |
| Ledge: | Roots: | Ledge: | Roots: | Ledge: | Roots: | Ledge: | Roots: |
| Restrictive: | | Restrictive: | | Restrictive: | | Restrictive: | |

**GROUNDWATER TABLE (near max., below max., etc.)** ______________

**SOIL MOISTURE (High, medium, low, etc.)** ______________

DATE: ______________ **PERCOLATION TEST DATA**

| **PERC:** | | **PERC:** | | **PERC:** | | **PERC:** | |
|---|---|---|---|---|---|---|---|
| **DEPTH:** | | **DEPTH:** | | **DEPTH:** | | **DEPTH:** | |
| **PRESOAK:** | | **PRESOAK:** | | **PRESOAK:** | | **PRESOAK:** | |
| **TIME** | **READING** | **TIME** | **READING** | **TIME** | **READING** | **TIME** | **READING** |
| | | | | | | | |
| **PERC RATE:** | | **PERC RATE:** | | **PERC RATE:** | | **PERC RATE:** | |

SITE INVESTIGATION FOR A SUBSURFACE SEWAGE DISPOSAL SYSTEM

North

**LOCATION DRAWING INCLUDING ALL TEST PITS AND PERCOLATION HOLES**

| SPECIAL CONDITIONS | | CONCLUSIONS | |
|---|---|---|---|
| Design Flow > 2000 GPD | | Suitable for Sewage Disposal | |
| Public Water Supply Watershed | | Unsuitable for Sewage Disposal | |
| Probable High Groundwater | | Additional Investigation Req'd | |
| Slope > 25 percent | | West Season Monitoring Req'd | |
| Perc Rate < 1 min/inch | | Retest During Wet Season | |
| Perc Rate > 30 min/inch | | Professional Engineer Plan Required | |
| Ledge < 5 feet below grade | | Other: | |
| Limited Suitable Area | | | |
| Open Watercourse or Wetland | | | |
| Flood Plain / Seasonal Flooding | | | |
| Max. G.W. < 36 inches below grade | | | |

**DESIGN RECOMMENDATIONS/COMMENTS**

________________________________________

________________________________________

________________________________________

________________________________________

Form completed by: ________________________________

(Director of Health/Sanitarian)

Witnessed by: ________________________________

Signature: ____________________ Owner ☐ Agent ☐ Date Signed: __________

Revised 1/31/2021

29 West Avenue
Essex, Connecticut 06426

Essex Health Department
www.essexct.gov

Phone: 860-767-4340 x118
Fax: 860-767-2019

# Application to Construct a NEW Septic System

**Fees:** ☐ Single-Family Residential $110.00 ☐ Restaurant $185.00 ☐ Commercial/Industrial $185.00
☐ Multi-Family Residential $185.00 ☐ Other Bldg. (describe): $185.00

**Plus soil testing fee as needed.** Includes ONE plan revision; additional plan revisions will be charged at one-half the original permit fee. All NEW subsurface sewage disposal systems in the Town of Essex shall require an engineered design. All applications must be accompanied by (2) proposal drawings at 1 inch to 20 ft. scale.

**Street Location** **Map** **Lot**

**Applicant Name** Phone
Address Email
Signature

**Property Owner Name** Phone
Address Email

**Engineer Name** Phone
Address Email
License #

**Installer Name** Phone
Address Email
Signature License # Expires

The installer MUST present a copy of his/her current license and sign the application IN PERSON

## Design Considerations

Soil Test (Date) Permit No ☐ Public Water Supply ☐ Private Well

**Area of Special Concern** (as per PHC 19-13-B103d(e) - check all that apply)

☐ Perc < 1min/inch ☐ Ground water <3 ft. ☐ Designated Wetland
☐ Perc >30min/inch ☐ Ledge < 5 ft. ☐ Area of Public Water Utility/Supply
☐ Slope >25% ☐ Soil limitations ☐ Within 100ft. of a watercourse/wetland/pond?
☐ Other ☐ Within 200ft. of a public water supply?

## Proposed Septic System

# Bedrooms: Tank Size: ☐ H-20 Tank ☐ Oversized Tub
Perc Rate: min/in Pump Chamber (size): ☐ H-20 Chamber ☐ Garbage Grinder
ELA Req'd SF Leaching Credit (SF/LF): Total Leaching (Length) LF
ELA Prov'd SF Leaching Structure: Length of Row 1 Row 2 .
Row 3 Row 4 .

Depth to Restrictive Layer: inches

MLSS: (HF) x (FF) x (PF) = LF (min. req'd length of each row)

☐ Footing Drain ☐ Curtain Drain ☐ Select Fill ☐ Other considerations

**Application #** **Date** **Fee Paid** **check #**

H:\- Forms\Health Dept Permit Applications\Construct NEW Septic System - Sept 2021.docx Rev. 9/2021

29 West Avenue
Essex, Connecticut 06426

Essex Health Department
www.essexct.gov

Phone: 860-767-4340 x118
Fax: 860-767-2019

## PERMIT TO CONSTRUCT A NEW SEPTIC SYSTEM
**FOR OFFICE USE ONLY**

**Street Location** ______________________ **Map** __________ **Lot** __________

**HEALTH DEPT. REVIEW DATE** ______________

Plan Date: ______________ ☐ CT DPH. Approval Req'd

1st Revision date: ______________ ☐ CT DEEP Approval Req'd

2nd Revision date: ______________ ☐ Central System Exception Req'd

**SPECIAL CONDITIONS**

☐ Water/Sewage Restriction ☐ Site Preparation

☐ Well Relocation/Retest ☐ Curtain Drain/Footing Drain

☐ Occupancy/Use Restriction ☐ Other: ______________

**COMMENTS:** ______________________________________________

Approval is hereby granted to construct a NEW septic system at ______________________

With the specifications and conditions described herein. There shall be no deviation from the specifications unless authorized by the sanitarian or his agent in writing.

**DATE ISSUED:** ______________ **This permit expires one year from the date of issuance.**

The **Installer** must contact the Essex Health Department and **give 48 hours of advanced notice** before beginning any septic installation or repair. Installation inspections are performed periodically by the Essex Health Department Inspector. The **licensed septic installer must be on site** during all phases of the installation. The Inspector keeps a detailed log of all inspections. A final inspection is required by the Inspector before the system is backfilled and covered. Once the installation is complete, and the Inspector has performed the final inspection, **the Engineer shall submit TWO copies of the AS-BUILT drawing** to the Health Department for review and approval. Once all requirements have been met, and the AS-BUILT drawing has been approved, a Permit to Discharge will be issued by the Health Department to the property owner.

**Health Dept. Approval:** ______________________________ ______________
Director of Health or Registered Sanitarian — Date

**Application #** __________ **Date** __________ **Fee Paid** __________ **check #** __________

**PLANNING AND ZONING COMMISSION**
**TOWN OF BRANFORD**
**1019 Main Street, Branford, CT 06405,**
**Telephone: (203) 488-1255, FAX: (203) 315-2188**

# APPLICATION FOR REVIEW OF COASTAL SITE PLANS

Supplemental Information for Projects Located Within the Coastal Boundary - -

Refer to coastal site plan application instruction sheet (attached) for sources of information and general comments pertinent to filling out this application.

APPLICANT'S NAME: ______________________ DATE: ____________

ADDRESS: ________________________________________________

PROJECT ADDRESS OR LOCATION: ______________________________

The following information must be supplied by the applicant and submitted in addition to, and along with, any application, plans and data required for approval of the proposed project under the zoning and/or subdivision regulations of this municipality. Attach additional sheets if more space is required.

## I. PLANS

### A. Project Plan(s)

This application must be accompanied by a plan (or plans) of the entire project indicating 1) project location, 2) design of all existing and proposed buildings, structures, and uses, 3) all proposed site improvements or alterations, and 4) ownership and type of use on adjacent properties.

### B. Coastal Resources

This application must be accompanied by a plan showing the locations of all coastal resources (as defined in section 3(1) of P.A. 79-535 on and contiguous to the site.

## II. WRITTEN INFORMATION

### A. Description of the Proposed Project

Describe the entire project including types of buildings and structures, uses, methods and timing of construction, type and extent of development adjacent to the site. This information should supplement and/or clarify plans in **1.A.** above.

________________________________________________

________________________________________________

________________________________________________

B. Description of Coastal Resources

Identify the coastal resources on and contiguous to the site (as shown on the coastal resources map) and describe their condition. This information should supplement and/or clarify the plan in I.B. above.

C. Assessment of the Suitability of the Project for the Proposed Site and the Capability of the Resources to Accommodate the Proposed Use

(1) Identify any and all coastal use policies (in section 2(b)(1) of P.A. 79-535 and reprinted in CAM Planning Report No. 30) applicable to the proposed project.

(2) Identify any and all coastal resource policies (in section 2(b) (2) of P.A. 79-535 and reprinted in CAM Planning Report No. 30) applicable to the proposed project.

(3) Describe how the proposed project is consistent with all of the coastal policies identified in C(1) and (2) above (i.e. describe the extent to which the project complies or conflicts with each policy). Note: if a project conflicts with any policy, the project should be modified to reduce or eliminate the conflict.

D. Evaluation of the potential Beneficial and Adverse Impacts of the Project and Description of Proposed Methods to Mitigate Adverse Effects.

(1) Identify and describe the potential adverse impacts (as defined in section 3(15) of P.A. 79-535) and potential beneficial impacts of the project on coastal resources.

For Waterfront Property Only:

(2) Is the project a water dependent use as defined in section 3(16) of P.A. 79-535? If so, explain why.

For Waterfront Property Only:

(3) Describe the impacts or effects (either positive or negative) that the project will have on future water dependent uses or development on and adjacent to this site.

(4) Describe the proposed measures to mitigate (reduce or eliminate any adverse impacts on coastal resources described in D(1) and, if applicable, on future water dependent development opportunities described in D (3).

E. <u>Demonstration of the Acceptability of Remaining or Unmitigated Adverse Impacts on Coastal Resources and Future Water Dependent Uses and Development</u>

(1) Describe any adverse impacts that remain after employing all reasonable mitigation measures.

_______________________________________________

_______________________________________________

(2) Explain why these remaining adverse impacts were not mitigated.

_______________________________________________

_______________________________________________

(3) Explain why the commission reviewing this application should find these remaining adverse impacts to be acceptable.

_______________________________________________

_______________________________________________

## III. SUPPORTING MATERIALS/DOCUMENTATION

A. The commission or board may request the submission of such additional information that it deems necessary in order to reach a decision on the application.

Include any additional information required by the commission and list any supplemental materials (plans, reports, etc.,) that are being submitted in support of this application.

| | |
|---|---|
| Owner______________________ | Applicant______________________ |
| PLEASE PRINT | PLEASE PRINT |
| Address______________________ | Address______________________ |
| Phone______________________ | Phone______________________ |
| E-mail______________________ | E-mail______________________ |
| Fax______________________ | Fax______________________ |
| Signature______________________ | Signature______________________ |

---

FOR OFFICE USE ONLY:

Receipt Date______________________ Fee Paid______________________

Approved/Denied by P&Z on______________________ Application #______________

Town of Branford
Building Department
Application for Residential Building Permit

**office use only**

Property Owner______________________________
Address______________________________
Town/City______________________ State________ Zip________
Phone Number______________ E-mail______________

Agent/Contractor Name______________________________
Address______________________________
Town/city______________________ State________ Zip________
Phone Number______________ E-mail______________
CT Registration Number______________ Exp.______________

**Property Information;**
Address of property where work is to be completed______________________________

☐ Public Sewer ☐ Private Septic ☐ Public Water ☐ Private Well

Property Located with Flood Hazard; ☐ Yes ☐ No ☐ Unknown

**Construction Information;**

☐ New ☐ Addition ☐ Alteration/Remodel ☐ Existing ☐ Other explain______________

☐ Single Family ☐ Two-Family ☐ Townhouse ☐ Multi-Family, Number of Units________

Area (sq. ft.) 1st floor________ 2nd floor________ 3rd floor________ Garage________ Deck________ Other________ Total________

Number of Bedrooms______ Number of Bathrooms________

Description and size of Proposed Work______________________________
______________________________
______________________________

Estimated Construction Cost including all labor and materials; ______________

By signing I hereby certify that I am the owner of record of the named property or that I have been authorized by the property owner of record to make this application as an authorized agent and we agree to conform to all applicable laws, regulations and town ordinances. All information contained within is true and accurate to the best of my knowledge and belief. No work shall be started until after the Town of Branford has approved and signed the applicant's permit application.

______________________ Date__________
Print Name

______________________
Signature owner/Authorized agent

---

**Do not print below this line Office use only**

Building permit fee______________ Permit Number______________
State Education______________
Document fee______________ Issued Date______________
Plans fee______________
Zoning fee______________ Approved by______________
Total Permit fee______________ Building Official or Designee

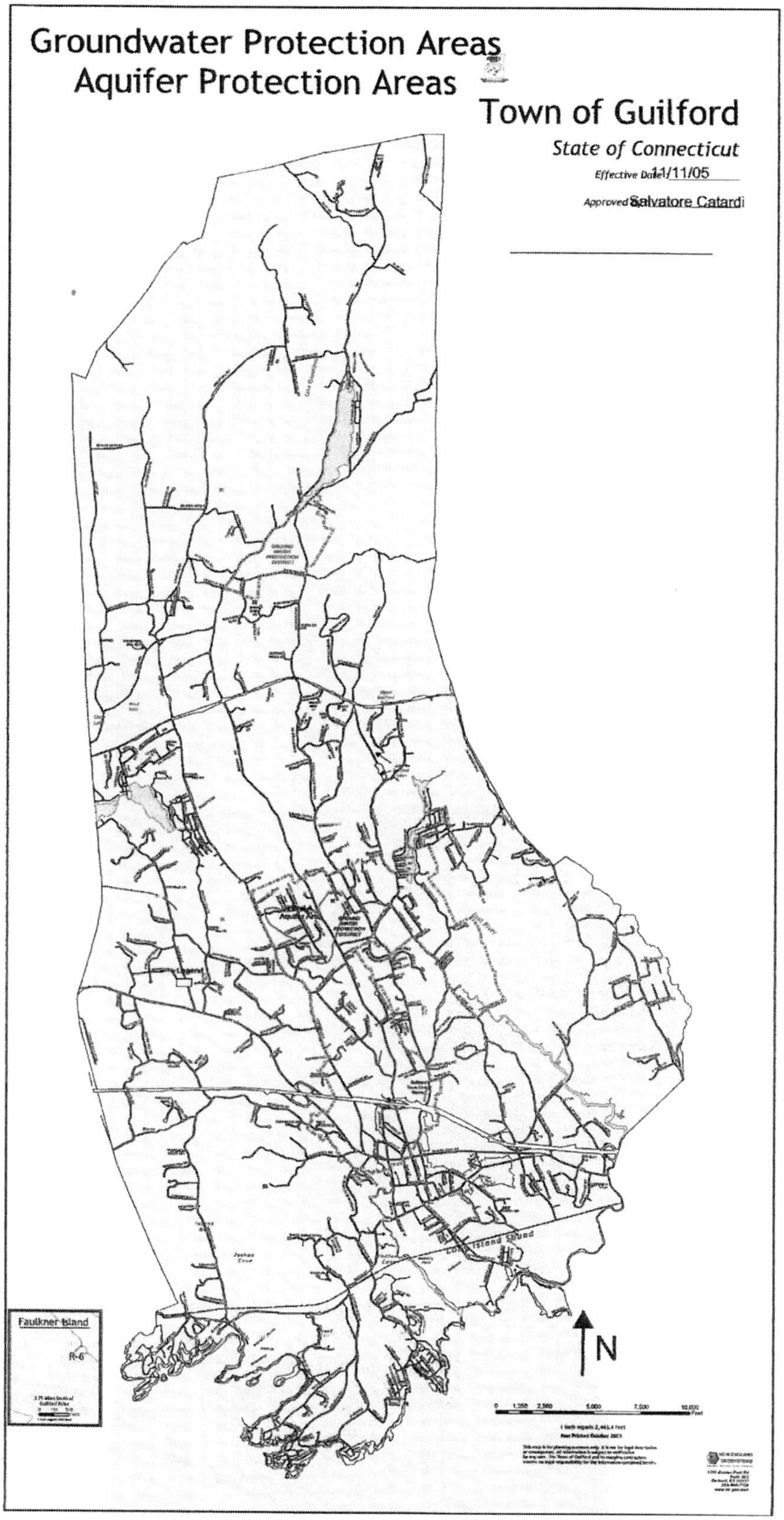
Groundwater Protection Areas
Aquifer Protection Areas
Town of Guilford
State of Connecticut
Effective Date 11/11/05
Approved Salvatore Catardi
Faulkner Island
R-6
Long Island Sound
N

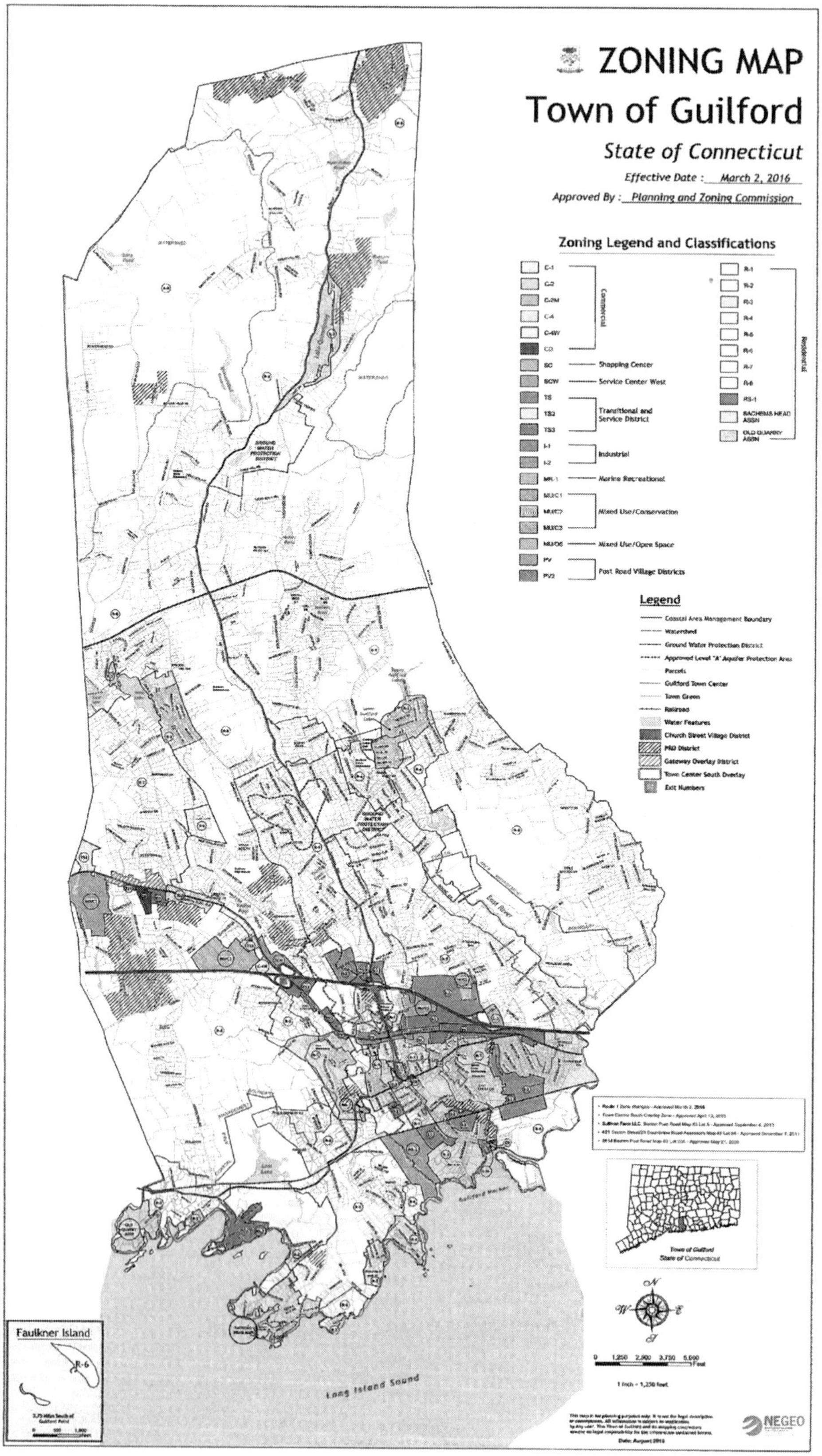
ZONING MAP
Town of Guilford
State of Connecticut
Effective Date : March 2, 2016
Approved By : Planning and Zoning Commission
Zoning Legend and Classifications
Commercial
Shopping Center
Service Center West
Transitional and Service District
Industrial
Marine Recreational
Mixed Use/Conservation
Mixed Use/Open Space
Post Road Village Districts
Residential
Legend
Coastal Area Management Boundary
Watershed
Ground Water Protection District
Approved Level "A" Aquifer Protection Area
Parcels
Guilford Town Center
Town Green
Railroad
Water Features
Church Street Village District
PRD District
Gateway Overlay District
Town Center South Overlay
Exit Numbers
Long Island Sound
Faulkner Island
R-6
1 inch = 1,250 feet
NEGEO

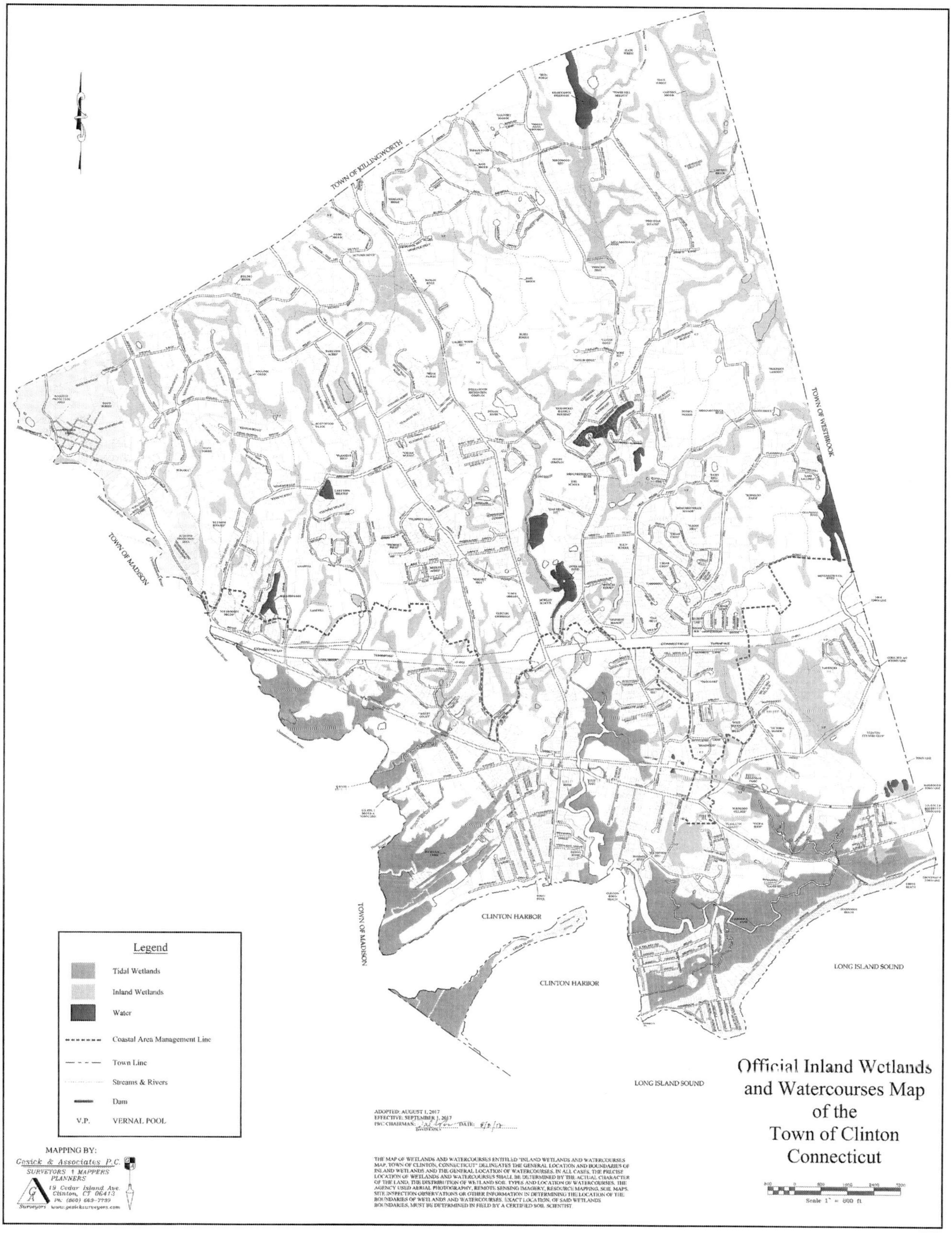
TOWN OF KILLINGWORTH
TOWN OF WESTBROOK
TOWN OF MADISON
TOWN OF MADISON
CLINTON HARBOR
CLINTON HARBOR
LONG ISLAND SOUND
LONG ISLAND SOUND
Legend
Tidal Wetlands
Inland Wetlands
Water
Coastal Area Management Line
Town Line
Streams & Rivers
Dam
V.P. VERNAL POOL
MAPPING BY:
Gesick & Associates P.C.
SURVEYORS + MAPPERS
PLANNERS
19 Cedar Island Ave.
Clinton, CT 06413
Ph: (860) 669-7799
Surveyors www.gesicksurveyors.com
ADOPTED: AUGUST 1, 2017
EFFECTIVE: SEPTEMBER 1, 2017
IWC CHAIRMAN: DATE:
THE MAP OF WETLANDS AND WATERCOURSES ENTITLED "INLAND WETLANDS AND WATERCOURSES MAP, TOWN OF CLINTON, CONNECTICUT" DELINEATES THE GENERAL LOCATION AND BOUNDARIES OF INLAND WETLANDS AND THE GENERAL LOCATION OF WATERCOURSES. IN ALL CASES, THE PRECISE LOCATION OF WETLANDS AND WATERCOURSES SHALL BE DETERMINED BY THE ACTUAL CHARACTER OF THE LAND, THE DISTRIBUTION OF WETLAND SOIL TYPES AND LOCATION OF WATERCOURSES. THE AGENCY USED AERIAL PHOTOGRAPHY, REMOTE SENSING IMAGERY, RESOURCE MAPPING, SOIL MAPS, SITE INSPECTION OBSERVATIONS OR OTHER INFORMATION IN DETERMINING THE LOCATION OF THE BOUNDARIES OF WETLANDS AND WATERCOURSES. EXACT LOCATION, OF SAID WETLANDS BOUNDARIES, MUST BE DETERMINED IN FIELD BY A CERTIFIED SOIL SCIENTIST.
Official Inland Wetlands
and Watercourses Map
of the
Town of Clinton
Connecticut
Scale 1" = 800 ft

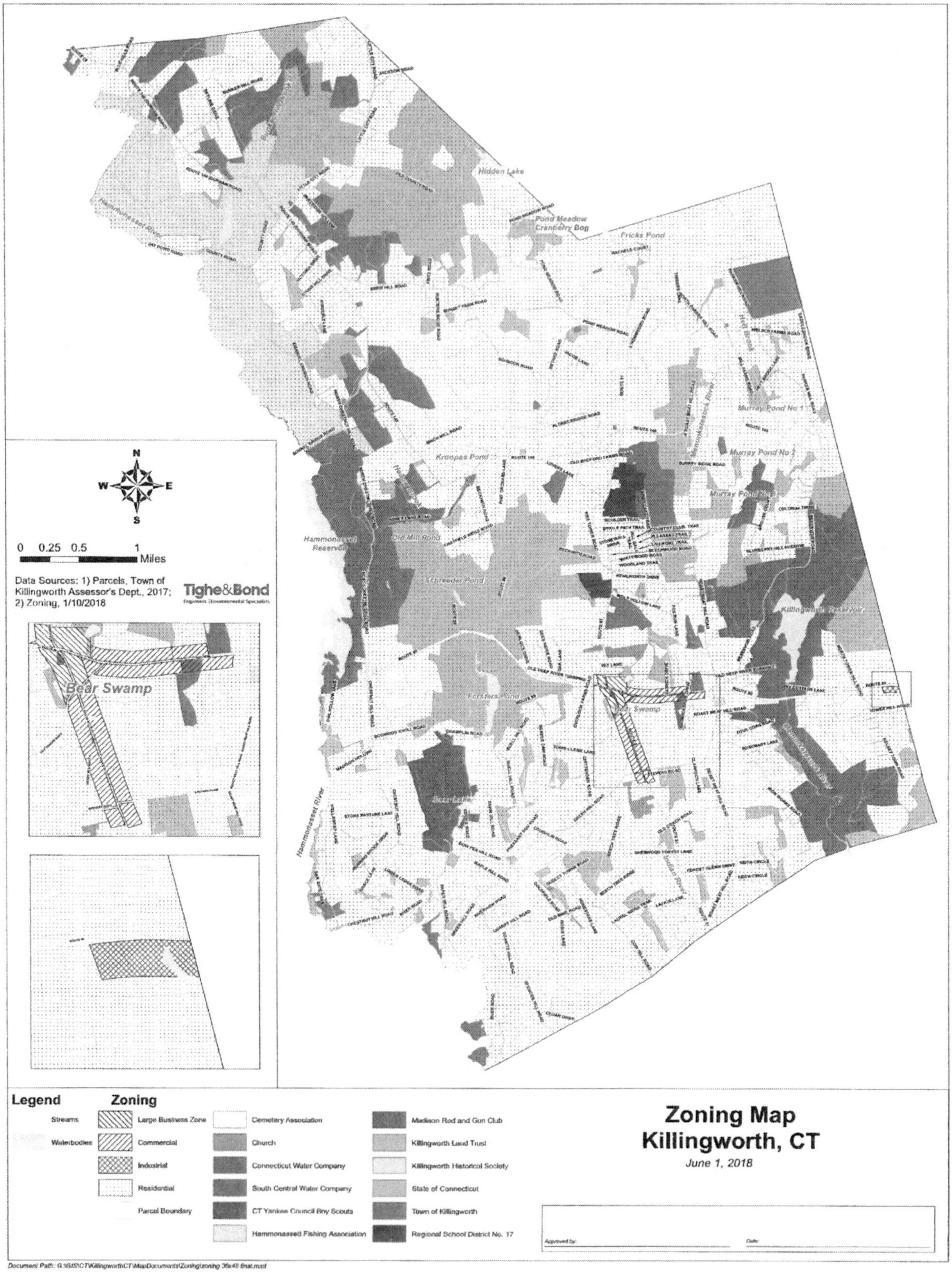


Document Path: G:\GIS\CT\KillingworthCT\MapDocuments\Zoning\zoning 36x48 final.mxd

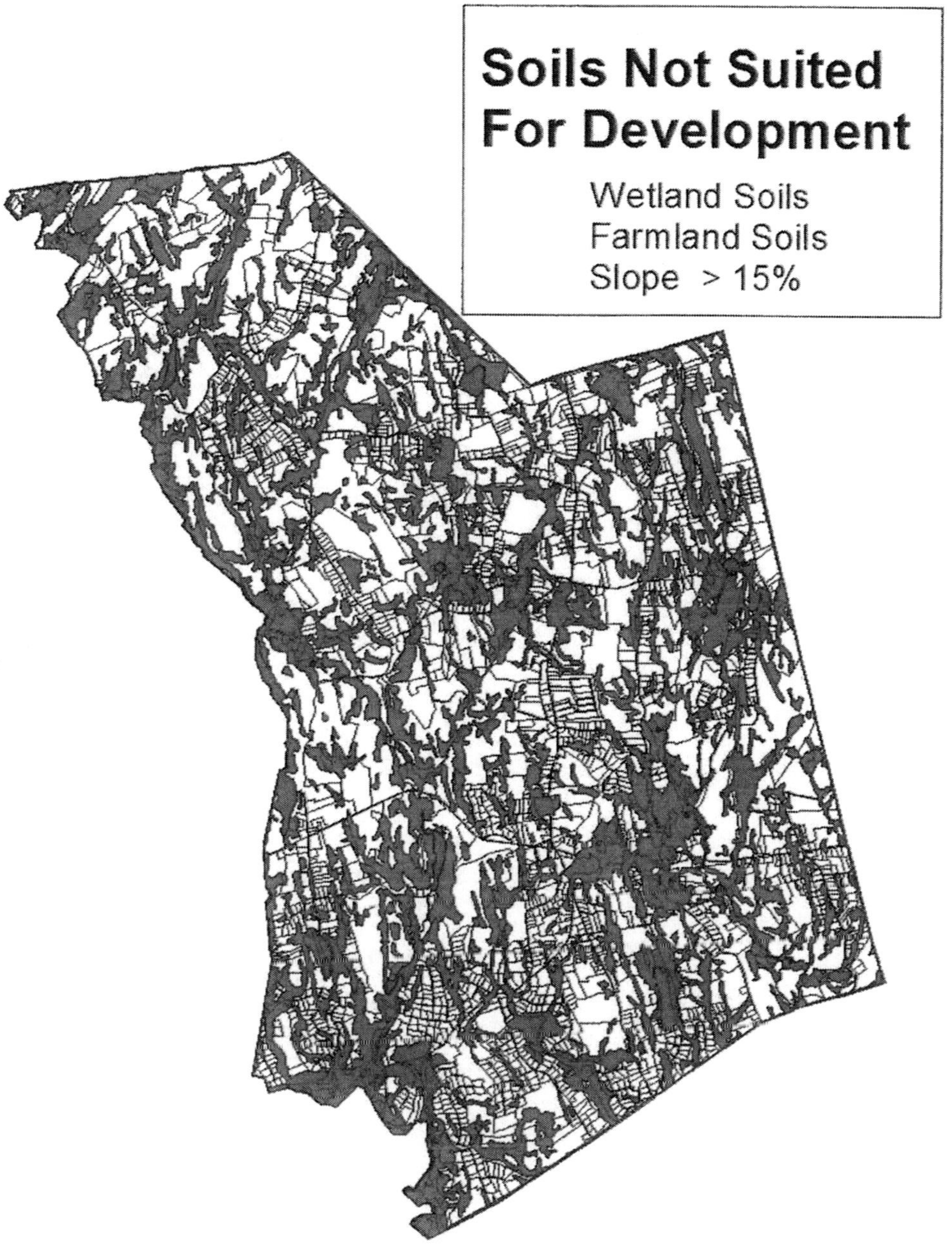


**Figure 1-10. Soils not suited for development.**

**4. Soils Not Suited for Development.** The map in Figure 1-10 is an aggregate of inland wetland, farmland, and steep slope soils shown in previous maps. All of these separate data layers are shown in red to indicate areas in Killingworth that may not be suited for development. The areas in white may be more suitable for development although some of these areas have soils with severe limitations for on-site septic systems.

# INDEX

**C**



**D**